INDIAN GRAPHIC NARRATIVES

CRITICAL RESPONSES

EDITED BY
SAPNA DOGRA

ATLANTIC
PUBLISHERS & DISTRIBUTORS (P) LTD

ATLANTIC
PUBLISHERS & DISTRIBUTORS (P) LTD
7/22, Ansari Road, Darya Ganj, New Delhi
Tel.: +91-11-4077 5252, 2327 3880
E-mail: orders@atlanticbooks.com
Web: www.atlanticbooks.com

Published by Atlantic Publishers & Distributors (P) Ltd 2024

Printed & bound in India by Atlantic Print Services

Dedicated to

My Parents

and

Professor Santosh K. Sareen

Acknowledgements

Editing a book is harder than I thought and more rewarding than I could have ever imagined. Nothing is ever the result of a single individual's effort. There are always so many active participants and silent supporters in the completion of a project. In this case, too, there were many, and I would like to thank them all.

I am eternally grateful to my literary agent, Mr. Suhail Mathur of The Book Bakers for helping me out in getting this book published.

My heartfelt thanks to Atlantic Publishers for approving the manuscript and accepting it for publication.

Professor Santosh K Sareen (retired, Jawaharlal Nehru University), my PhD guide, for his guidance, encouragement, and friendship.

The support of my husband Sandeep who encourages me to venture into almost everything.

My son Samaksh for his endless faith and love.

My parents who taught me discipline, love, gratitude, respect, and so much more that has helped me succeed in life.

I want to thank EVERYONE who ever said anything positive to me or taught me something.

To all my contributors, a heartfelt THANK YOU.

Contents

Introduction

Even though comics have always been a favourite of children throughout the world, it is only recently that graphic novels, which are an extended narrative version of comics, have caught up with adult readers. Since any graphic narrative is an amalgamation of the visual and the verbal, it mirrors our times that are saturated with images. Stephen E. Tabachnick in the introduction to *The Cambridge Companion to The Graphic Novel* (2017) says,

> Teachers no less than their students are excited because the graphic novel has attracted extremely talented writers and artists, and they have rendered powerful narratives, going far beyond the previous newspaper comics' light entertainment, superhero adventures, and children's stories. While they employ the same techniques as traditional comics, graphic novel's production values are much better, their content is much more complex and sophisticated, and (despite the obvious meaning of graphic "novel") they include non-fiction as well as fiction. It is now clear that there is no subject too profound or complex for the graphic novel to treat. . .(1)

Ever since the publication of the Pulitzer Prize winner *Maus* by Art Spiegelman in 1986 which recounted the holocaust of World War II, graphic novels have become an attractive medium to voice the concerns of the oppressed and the marginalised everywhere. The very first graphic novel from India, *River of Stories* (1994) by Orijit Sen, had an ecological concern. It traced the Narmada Bachao Andolan and the construction of dams across the river Narmada that displaced thousands of natives of that area.

Today, the stage had been set for more artists to join in. The more recent graphic novelists like Sarnath Banerjee and Vishwajyoti Ghosh followed the footsteps of Sen and have been successful with readers in India. From *Amar Chitra Katha*, the comic book series, to the reworking of mythologies as in Amruta Patil's *Adi Parva: Churning of the Ocean* (2012), *Sauptik: Blood and Flowers* (2016) and *Aranyaka: Book of the Forest* (2019), Indian graphic narratives have come a long way. Pramod K. Nayar in *Indian Graphic Novel: Nation, History and Critique* (2016) says,

> The texts have debated history and historical events like the Partition, social issues such as caste, development and child abuse, documented lives and satirized contemporary Indian culture. The graphic narrative, in the English language in India, is thus constitutive, like Indian literature, of Indian *urban* social imaginaries among the English-speaking classes to which it offers alternate readings of India history, draws attention to the lacunae and follies of our cultural practices and makes visible hitherto taboo subjects (7).

The "Indian *urban* social imaginaries" as pointed out by Nayar constitutes homosexuality as in Amruta Patil's *Kari* (2008); the Indian Emergency of 1975–1977 in Vishwajyoti Ghosh's *Delhi Calm* (2010); child sexual abuse in Pratheek Thomas's *Hush* (2010); caste discrimination in Srividya Natrajan and S. Anand's *Bhimayana: Experiences of Untouchability* (2011) and Srividya Natrajan and Aparajita Ninan's *A Gardener in the Wasteland: Jyotiba Phule's Fight for Liberty* (2011); scarring memories in Vishwajyoti Ghosh's *This Side, That Side: Restorying Partition* (2013); dystopian water wars in Sarnath Banerjee's *All Quiet in Vikaspuri* (2015), political situation of Kashmir in Malik Sajad's *Munnu: A Boy from Kashmir* (2015), sexuality and gender in Priya Kuriyan's anthology of graphic stories, *Drawing the Line: Indian Women Fight Back* (2015), to name a few.

The Indian graphic narrative is becoming an integral part of the canon of Indian Writing in English (IWE). Nayar (2016) says that graphic narratives add "to the existing corpus of texts in Indian Writing in English a new representational mode that re-invigorates the canon, the form and the themes". He further adds that graphic narratives highlight the conflicts and challenges of traditional IWE and "discusses these in popular medium, offering therefore, not only a democratizing of forms of socio-political commentary but also a democratizing of the language of cultural analytics" (7).

What distinguishes graphic novels from comics are length, serialisation, seriousness or authenticity, cartoonicity of the characters and complexity (Hescher 2016, 3). There also happens to be confusion with words like comics, graphic literature, graphic novel, graphic fiction, and graphic narrative, which are often used interchangeably. Nayar (2016) has something interesting to add to this debate:

> I see the term 'graphic literature' as inadequate due to its emphasis on words – 'literature' – and I definitely do not wish to use the term 'comics' due to the emphasis on the 'cartoony' or 'funnies' that the term is semantically loaded with. . .The term 'graphic novel', often mocked by practitioners of the form like Frank Miller, is the extended version of the comics, and mainly fictional in scope and theme. . .a better term would be graphic *narrative*. . . 'Graphic narrative' as a descriptor and label references both the visual component of the medium ('graphic') as the crafting and telling of a story ('narrative') (4–5).

Thus, this volume uses the term graphic narrative as an all-inclusive term that encompasses narratives that deploy the amalgamation of the verbal and the visual.

Chapters in this Volume

The first chapter, 'The Graphic Deterritorialisation: A Socio-Analytic Study of Amruta Patil's *Kari*' by Dr. Ambika Sharma, is a philosophical engagement with Amruta Patil's *Kari* (2008), where the protagonist is a deterritorialised self—both culturally and geographically. The article throws light on the identity crisis, self-estrangement, social isolation and the search for a tangible meaning of existence. *Kari* not only problematises the issues of being a queer woman but also portrays a woman who is divided between the normative and the not-so-normative belief systems.

The second chapter, 'Gender and Violence in Graphic Narratives in India' by Sandhya Nayak, examines representations of gender-based violence in recent graphic narratives from India. The focus is on the lesbian relationship and related issues in *Kari* (2008) by Amruta Patil and on being a woman living in turbulent times in India in *Drawing the Line: Indian Women Fight Back* (2015)—an anthology of graphic narratives edited by Priya Kurian, Larissa Bertonasco and Ludmilla Bartscht. The texts show a modern India changing according to the needs of the times. Both texts portray very strong and self-aware women who are willing to take up the challenges and obstacles that society throws at them. *Kari* brings the traditional Indian woman out of the closet and traces her transformation into a bold person, who is not ashamed to disclose her homosexuality. *Drawing the Line: Indian Women Fight Back* is an anthology of stories about women who have a never say die attitude through the harrowing pain and violence that they undergo. The paper attempts to examine the depiction of women in recent works in comparison with Indian comics and graphic narratives that were produced around fifty years ago, further analyzing the grounds for the occurrence of rapid change in these representations.

Storytelling is an art, and this art of sequentially narrating a story through graphics has become a popular medium of expression. Thus, graphic narratives are a viable medium for exploring social, political and individual issues. *Corridor (2004)* by Sarnath Banerjee is one such witty, satirical graphic novel that lays bare society's preconceived notions and paradigms and how it affects the lives of the individual. Society has a pivotal role to play in determining an individual's behavioral patterns and goes a long way in determining their individuality. The aim of the third chapter, 'The Impact of Social Paradigms and its Resonance on the Characters of *Corridor* by Sarnath Banerjee' written by Smita Dabi, is to explore the viabilities of these paradigms on the lives of the characters of the novel *Corridor*. It assesses and establishes the significance of society's expectations in terms of certain categorised behaviour from individuals. This impact has been assessed in terms of social, political and even personal context, resulting in psychological turmoil and perplexity over one's individuality. The narrative techniques of the author in the exploration of the same have also been assessed.

The fourth chapter, 'Cityscapes and Real-Imagined Spatiality: Locating Topophrenia in Amruta Patil's *Kari*' by Nidhi Sharma, looks at space as a complex expression that is social, metaphysical as well as personal. *Kari* is a rich graphic novel that can be looked upon as a map that surveys geographies of the smog city and uses locations with shadings of real and fictive coordinates. The narrative of the novel functions as a way to examine how the titular protagonist's flaneuring invites varied ways of seeing the metro city through a gender-fluid sensibility. The idea of 'evolving space' (Massey 2005) becomes an interesting point of investigation in a graphic text like this, where pictures and words open interpretations of spaces and places through the stories told through them. Through a literary cartographic approach, several spaces like oppressive home, sewage and cityscapes can be seen through topophrenic sensibilities that reorient our understanding of lived places. Topophrenia is a necessary condition of 'identifiable place mindedness', allied with a condition of dis-ease. It captures people's experience of places they hate or fear (Tally 2018). *Kari's* metaspace, with the juxtaposition of fact and fiction, is informed by a topophrenic inclination that arises out of her standing up against heteronormativity and the flaming walls of sexuality. The paper explores places like a referent and then moves on to study the oscillation (as imbibed in the notion of topophrenia) between the place and its representation to open newer avenues of space in this graphic text.

The fifth chapter, 'Psychological Trauma Through Efficacious Visualisation: A Study of *Hush*' by S. Sri Sakuntala, is a study of Pratheek Thomas' *Hush* (2010). It is a wordless graphic novel that speaks only through pictures. Since pictures speak louder than words, *Hush* effectively voices the voiceless victim of sexual abuse. Sexual violence has far-reaching consequences that go far beyond physical injuries, regardless of age or gender. The trauma of being sexually assaulted or raped can be life changing. It could leave one feeling terrified, ashamed, alone and plagued by nightmares, flashbacks and other unpleasant memories. The way of representing the story through efficacious drawings helps the study and envision a story with the utmost attention.

The sixth chapter, 'Amruta Patil's *Kari*: Marginalised Non-Heterosexual in Normalised Heterosexual Metropolitan City' by M. Sri Varshni and Dr. V. Sunitha, analyses the concept of gender performativity in Amrutha Patil's groundbreaking work, *Kari* (2008). The queer protagonist, Kari, articulates her gender fluidity in a heteronormative society. *Kari* pictures the life of a girl who bears the burden of being non-binary in a normalised heterosexual metropolitan city, which is referred to as the smog city throughout the novel. This paper focuses on the heteronormative culture in a metropolitan city and the problematic portrayal of homosexuals as unnatural. The image of darkness, sewer and inner fox uncovers social marginalisation based on sexuality.

In this fast-paced, technology-driven world, digitalisation has contributed to the soaring success of human civilisation in almost every field. At the same time, it has also left behind a few faithful friends. Books happen to be one of them. With the arrival of multimedia and easy internet access, books quickly lost their sheen and appeal to their readers. Thus, it is quite ironic that once considered a milestone in the road to development, these pieces of literature are now branded as obsolete and tedious by the new generation. Therefore, the need of the hour is to refurbish it according to the requirements of modern times. The advent of graphic books in the Indian literary scene seems to be promising in this regard. It makes use of the best of both worlds by coalescing literature with images. Despite this, academicians are afraid that it would hamper a student's language skills in the formative stages. Though their fears are not completely unfounded, if applied with caution, these graphic books would do wonders in the case of reluctant readers. The requisite action would be, therefore, to analyze its pros and cons, thereby tapping its extensive potential for the betterment of the students in future. The seventh chapter,

'Graphic Narratives: An Innovative Tool to Educate and Inspire' by Darakhshan Niyaz, explores these issues.

The eighth chapter, 'Graphic Narratives: An Emerging Source of Education for Learners' by Dr. Ritu Pareek, attempts to discuss the history of graphic narratives in India and present the perspectives of teachers to highlight the existing scenario. It showcases the interest of the students in including graphic narratives as a medium and source to facilitate them with moral and educational values.

The ninth chapter, 'Animals as Visual Metaphors in Graphic Narratives' by Dr. Sapna Dogra, looks at anthropocentrism as a literary technique that achieves an ecstatic outcome. Art Spiegelman's Holocaust graphic novel, *Maus* (1986) recounted the tale of Spiegelman's father, Vladek Spiegelman, an Auschwitz survivor. It is a daringly political novel that uses the imagery of mice as Jews, cats as Nazis and dogs as Americans. *Munnu: A Boy from Kashmir* (2015) by Malik Sajad presents the Kashmiris as the critically endangered Hangul deer (or Kashmiri stag). This paper seeks to answer why it is easier to make a point using animal characters, rather than their human counterpart. Anthropocentrism adds to the aesthetic presentation and establishes structure and agency. In turn, this generates and constructs an interspace separate from reality, a space that furnishes the necessary distance for the reader. It also achieves the 'alienation effect' as propounded by German playwright, Bertot Brecht (1964).

Naseer Ahmed, who lives in Srinagar, wrote the graphic novel *Kashmir Pending* in 2007. It addresses regional unrest and chronicles the story of numerous people in Kashmir. The protagonist, Mushtaq, proceeds to tell the tale of his life, from his birth in 1971 to his radicalisation, incarceration and reconciliation while sitting in the dark yet tranquil shadows of his prison cell. It is a grim narrative that shows the futility of violence. The novel is a critique of the violence of manipulation inflicted upon the young Kashmiris. The last chapter, 'Violence and Manipulation in *Kashmir Pending*' by Dr. Sapna Dogra, investigates the disciplinary institutions of power and monitoring used by the Indian government. The novel offers a counter-narrative and aids in dispelling the liberal idea that India is a nation-state with a uniform and representative democratic process. Such literary texts lay bare the violent tactics used by the military to assert its supremacy over the area it deems vulnerable and disturbed. The paper argues that Singh's *Kashmir Pending* refuses to take sides and presents the situation in Kashmir in shades of grey.

Considering the various issues that the present book discusses and explores, it becomes imperative to accept that "The Indian graphic narrative must be seen as a part of this global 'graphic turn' to stories of disaster, diseases, deprivation and displacement, stories that constitute the foundational texts of global campaigns for rights, equality and end of suffering. Thus, the Indian graphic narrative is poised to become a part of the *global popular*, taking *specific local contexts and conditions of casteism or abuse via a globally hypervisible and widely recognized medium, onto the world readership screens*." (Nayar 2016, 197)

Hopefully, this volume will be of use to teachers, students and researchers who wish to unravel this exciting new area of artistic expression.

Dr. Sapna Dogra

Works Cited

Ahmed, Naseer. 2007. *Kashmir Pending*. New Delhi: Phantomville.

Banerjee, Sarnath. 2001. *Barn Owl's Wondrous Capers*. New Delhi: Penguin.

———. 2004. *Corridor.* New Delhi: Penguin Books.

———. 2011. *The Harappan Files*. New Delhi: Harper Collins.

———. 2015. *All Quiet in Vikaspuri*. New Delhi: Harper Collins.

Brecht, Bertolt, and Eric Bentley. 1961. "On Chinese Acting." *The Tulane Drama Review* 6 (1): 130–36. https://doi.org/10.2307/1125011.

Ghosh, Vishwajyoti. 2010. *Delhi Calm*. New Delhi: Harper Collins.

———. 2013. *This Side, That Side: Restorying Partition*. New Delhi: Yoda Press.

Hescher, Achim. 2016. *Reading Graphic Novels: Genre and Narration*. Berlin, Boston: De Gruyter.

Kuriyan, Priya et al. (eds.). 2016. *Drawing the Line: Indian Women Fight Back*. New Delhi: Zubaan.

Massey, Doreen. 2005. *For Space*. SAGE Publications Limited.

Natarajan, Srividya, and Aparajita Ninan. 2011. *A Gardener in the Wasteland*. New Delhi: Navayana.

Natarajan, Srividya and S. Anand. 2011. *Bhimayana: Experiences of Untouchability*. New Delhi: Navyana.

Nayar, Pramod. K. 2016. *The Indian Graphic Novel: Nation, History and Critique*. London: Routledge.

Patil, Amruta. 2008. *Kari*. India: Harper Collins.

———. 2016. *Sauptik: Blood and Flower*. India: Harper Collins.

———. 2012. *Adi Parva: Churning of the Ocean*. India: Harper Collins.

———. 2019. *Aranyaka: Book of the Forest*. India: Westland.

Sajad, Malik. 2015. *Munnu: A Boy from Kashmir*. India: Fourth Estate.

Sen, Orijit. 1994. *The River of Stories*. New Delhi: Kalpavriksh.

Spiegelman, Art. 1986. *Maus*. New York: Pantheon Books.

Tabachnick, Stephen E. (ed). 2017. *The Cambridge Companion to The Graphic Novel*. UK: Cambridge University Press.

Tally, Robert T., Jr. 2018. *Topophrenia: Place, Narrative, and the Spatial Imagination*. Indiana University Press.

Thomas, Pratheek and Rajiv Eipe. 2011. *Hush*. Bangalore: Manta Ray Comics.

List of Contributors

Sapna Dogra, Deputy Chief Editor of *Muse India* (ISSN: 0975-1815) is an Assistant Professor (English) in the Department of Higher Education, Government of Himachal Pradesh. Email: sapnardm@gmail.com

Ambika Sharma is an Assistant Professor of English, Department of Humanities and Social Sciences, National Institute of Technology, Hamirpur, Himachal Pradesh. Email: ambikasharmarr656@gmail.com

Sandhya Nayak is an Assistant Professor of English at St Agnes UG College, Mangalore. Email: sandhyapai@stagnescollege.edu.in

Smita Dabi is pursuing her PhD from Banasthali Vidyapith Rajasthan. Email: smita.dabi@gmail.com

Nidhi Sharma is an Assistant Professor of English in the Department of English at SGND Khalsa College, University of Delhi. Email: nidhisharma21@gmail.com

S. Sri Sakuntala is a research scholar at Koneru Lakshmaiah Education Foundation, Vaddeswaram, Guntur, Andhra Pradesh. Email: ssrishakuntala@gmail.com

M. Sri Varshni is pursuing her PhD in English at the Vellore Institute of Technology, Vellore, Tamil Nadu. Email: srivarshnimuthukrishnan10@gmail.com

V. Sunitha is an Assistant Professor Senior in the Department of English, School of Social Sciences and Languages at Vellore Institute of Technology, Vellore, Tamil Nadu.

Darakhshan Niyaz is an Assistant Professor, Department of English, Digboi Mahila Mahavidyalaya, Assam. Email: dnashraf333@gmail.com

Ritu Pareek is an Assistant Professor, Birla Institute of Technology, Mesra, Jaipur Campus, Rajasthan. Email: rituparee k@bitmesra.ac.in

1

The Graphic Deterritorialisation: A Socio-Analytic Study of Amruta Patil's *Kari*

Ambika Sharma

Introduction

In the Deleuzian sense, the desire of being and becoming is not a matter of fixity but a matter of pertinent flow. These flows often emanate from the dominant centres of society and sometimes lead to the deterritorialisation of the self. The desire to reterritorialise oneself becomes a constant tussle on the part of the self. Life crisis often acts as the precursor for the emergence of alienation; both intrinsically and extrinsically. Alienation, in its varied forms, can be found within the matrix of literature that is existentialist. Modern fiction often renders insights into isolational fragmentation—a desire towards the becoming of a being. Many texts deal with alienation as a pertinent thematic stance. Some texts show alienated protagonists shifting both spaces and places. This shifting occurs from indulgence to negotiation to the realisation of existential lure. Modern fiction peers through the prism of baffled statehood, wherein different personalities are often seen searching for their true identities—culturally as well as geographically. The inquisitive mind over the years seeks to question the ebbs and flows of the cosmos of life, the relevance of one's living, the cause of one's birth and death in an ungrateful world where everyone has to run for their life, that too bare feet. The meaning of life is decoded from existential graves of thoughts, where the immanent being is dislocated and lost.

The core paradox of the modern era is that interactions these days are online. This is the era of social connectivity and digital production. We live in a world more connected than ever, but the opposite is equally true. We are lonelier than ever, more depressed and anxious than ever. The reason that alienation carries the baggage of serious consequences is that a human being is a social animal—an assemblage of bodies in a territory or on a plane. In the Deleuzian sense, all life and its meanings are a plane of becoming. The perception of the fixed entity here, that is, man, is an effect of becoming.

Alienation is a subjective feeling, a feeling that people are not with us, don't understand us and we don't feel connected to anyone. It is different from social isolation. Some people can have a wide network of people around their lives and still feel deterritorialised. They stand broken from the connected wholes of becoming.

In the ethological sense, a territory is that which epitomises an environment constituted by beings and their frequent interactions. It is representative of a site that showcases the becoming of one, a site where belongingness is cultural, geographical and psychological. This territorial site is often covered with the geography of thoughts that give and assign labels and tags in a heteronormative society. Thoughts that may lead to alienation, which may then lead to the grave of existentialist dilemmas. This article throws light on the identity crisis, self-estrangement, social isolation and the search for a tangible meaning of existence, as depicted through the homosexual and queer protagonist in Amruta Patil's 2008 graphic novel, *Kari*. If we dig deep into the various events of the novel, we can find a clear insight into the character being a deterritorialised self—both culturally and geographically.

In the beginning, the book showcases the double suicide of the lesbian lovers—Kari and Ruth. The parting away of the lovers brings out the turmoil inflicted upon the protagonist, Kari, wherein we witness how in a heterosexual world, she not only finds herself cornered but also deterritorialised. The heterosexual culturalscapes of the metropolitan world suffocate the immanent self of Kari in the smog city of Mumbai.

From Territorialised Self to the Deterritorialised Self

Developed in the twentieth century, the philosophy of existentialism focuses on the questions of human existence and the ways in which humans deal with their existence in the world. It began in the nineteenth century with the philosophy of Soren Kierkegaard, who is regarded as the Father of Existentialism. It claims that humans define their own meaning in life. Popularised by two great French writers, Jean-Paul Sartre and Albert Camus, existentialism gained popularity after World War II, as the horrors of the holocaust led many people to abandon their beliefs in an ordered world. This despair has been communicated well by the philosophers of the late twentieth century and even continues to be a popular way of dealing with life in the twenty-first century. Simply stated, existentialism exchanges view about finding the meaning of life through the means of free will, choice and personal responsibility. It means pertaining to one's existence, externally driven and internally drawn. Its mantra is to claim that existence precedes essence. In other words, our birth, that is, existence, happens first. Then, it is up to each of us to determine who we are and write our essence through the way we choose to live. According to Sartre (2007), "We mean that man first of all exists, encounters himself, surges up and defines himself afterwards" (290). The prevailing belief is that people are in continuous search of finding meaning in their lives as they make choices based on their experiences and beliefs. Consequently, the traces of existentialism immediately entered the orb of literature. Indian novels are very rich in the depiction of existential motifs, keeping par with reality. Modern Indian literature offers a very clear picture of man's existential dilemmas of being and becoming.

The Graph of the Graphic Narrative Genre

The graphic narrative today has become a popular genre. It offers a picture to its readers wherein they should look beyond the graphic frame of the subject and the subjects. Over the past few decades, a recently developed form of the graphic novel has reshaped the scenario of Indian comics, including both scene and sense. Orijit Sen has been the first artist to have introduced the genre into the realm of Indian English literature with his first graphic novel, *River of Stories* (1994). A graphic frame that serves to highlight the controversies associated with the Narmada dam movement in India. In the last two decades, a wide number of graphic frames have been born on Indian soil. There have been the likes of Sarnath Banerjee's *Corridor* (2004), Amruta Patil's *Kari* (2008), Vishwajyoti Ghosh's renowned 2010 novel, *Delhi Calm* and the life story of B.R. Ambedkar in *Bhimayana: Experiences of Untouchability* (2011) by Srividya Natrajan and S. Anand. Every graphic text offers a unique graphic frame to be deconstructed. Thus, the traditional and historical graphic literature, like the religious *Amar Chitra Katha* (1967) and the very famous *Chacha Chaudhary* (1971), now stands overshadowed by these propounders of novelty, bringing forth the real issues of our social frame of thought and manners, of life and being, of being and becomings.

Amruta Patil's debut novel, *Kari*, was published when the first wave of graphic novels started, along with other ground-breaking works. It is different in the manner of presenting a queer protagonist who stands deterritorialised, both culturally and geographically. This innovative graphic offering by Amruta Patil breaks away from the cliché of the traditional narratives, as we witness *Kari* being the journey of a lesbian woman by a woman artist.

Kari's Cultural / Geographical Estrangement

Amruta Patil's much-acclaimed graphic novel, *Kari*, is also existential, in which the emotional side of the protagonist has been analysed. The very meaning of the self and the other is derived from our connectivities of the social arena, which we inhabit or are a part of. In this process, our desires act as the machinic forces that turn us to become desiring machines. The protagonist, *Kari,* too, falls prey to the notions of desire—a desire for home and belongingness. However, as the graph of this graphic novel proceeds, we witness Kari as somebody who eventually becomes a paranoid social machine—listening to the forces outside and not within. She is the victim of isolating graphs, to which she is subjected time and again. As a result, she stands deterritorialised from her body, her being, her desires, all of it.

Kari is a migrant in the suburban city of Mumbai, trying to bring her life back on track. She is an unusual protagonist, a young, deeply introverted, asocial, and queer woman who is trying to get out of the pit of her homosexuality after a recent breakup. The novel revolves around Kari and her sense of 'being' that arises due to her separation from her lover Ruth. Kari is a lesbian who has a beautiful relationship with Ruth. They are subjected to a breakup right at the beginning of the novel. After this breakup, Kari drowns deep into the world of isolation against the world of the normative order. This leads to her cultural deterritorialisation. The novel unfolds with the attempted double suicide of two lovers: Kari and Ruth. Kari committed suicide by jumping off a tall building and falling right into a sewer and "was saved by a sewer, by the stinking river" (Patil 2008, 8). Her relationship with Ruth helped her realise her dream of establishing a family. However, her desires for love and family are both shattered due to the heterosexual societal norms, which eventually lead to her deterritorialised schizoid self. Gilles Deleuze points out that the very forces that lead to one's territorialisation can sometimes act in reversal and lead to one's deterritorialised sense of being.

The validation that is enjoyed by heterosexuality in society is presented in the novel with the help of many instances; one such instance is a conversation between Kari and the two permanent guests of her apartment—Orgo and Zap. They advise Kari to discover a normal order in her sexuality and to look for a good man she can start her life with. There is another such instance when her very friendly colleague Lazarus questions her very bluntly about her sexuality, "Are you, like, a proper lesbian?" (Patil 2008, 79). This question, which seems to everyone almost okay to ask, reflects the standardisation of heterosexuality in our society, where people with non-heterosexual desires and behaviours are inherently labelled. People with same-sex desires are generally marginalised and stigmatised by society. Society, with its inherent notions, outrightly declares homosexuality as an immoral, unhealthy and freely chosen vice. Kari is forcibly alienated because of her homosexuality. Patil uses the negative connotations of the words sewer and stench to highlight the plight of her protagonist and the mentality of the social order of which she is a part. Patil is trying to make a connection between her protagonist and the sewer in the city, wherein the sewer is a symbol of something cornered and deterritorialised, much like Kari.

Kari works in an ad agency in Mumbai and lives in a rented apartment with two roommates. She often talks about her way back home and the choking nature of the smog city:

> I try to breathe as little as I can to prevent smog city from choking me. I wish I could detach my lungs. Every day, the city seems to be getting heavier, and her varicose veins fight to break out of her skin. Soon we must mutate – thick skins and resilient lungs – to survive this new reality (Patil 2008, 13).

The sewer saved her from her imminent death when she tried to end her life by jumping off a skyscraper. That day, she promised to pay back the favour by unclogging the drainage of the sewer. One fine night, Kari earns herself a boat and rows clean through the darkest water. She cleans the water. Having no one emotionally attached to her, she develops an emotional relationship with the sewer. The idea of sewer always remains in her mind: "washing the stench off my body when I get back home is a ritual. I can see the stench, eager as mercury, rush into the drain hole to join the mother bog" (Patil 2008, 34).

A few days later, on her way back home, she smells the stench again as if the sewer is reminding her of its existence, "Hello, grins the sewer, I am still here" (Patil 2008, 41). Kari imagines the city's digestive system to be so unwell that it has poisoned the water. Deleuze in *Capitalism and Schizophrenia* (2013) points out this chaos. He writes that when spaces stand deterritorialised, bodies are thrown out into a mudhole of instability. Patil's deep interpretation of the deterritorialisation of self, desires and being is further supported by the term self-estrangement. Self-estrangement is an alternate form of alienation that is commonly associated with post-modern society. In this novel, Kari is being estranged with special forms of social isolation. She often feels lonely and marginalised, even in the place where she is living. What follows is a geographical deterritorialisation. She lives in a 2BHK flat with her roommates, Billo and Delna, who are visited regularly by their boyfriends, Zap and Orgo. However, with several people in one apartment, Kari still does not feel sheltered. She is somewhere sandwiched between the lives of two couples, "Although I am not part of the organism, they like me well enough" (Patil 2008, 23). Additionally, she is sandwiched between places as well. Being a migrant in the city, she is completely oblivious to reality and is left to face the harsh dilemmas of the city and the self. If one looks beyond the greyscales of the graphic visuals of the text, the spaces appear to be full of morbidity.

In Spinozian terminology, the body is what is endless, for it just does not comprise what is within but that which falls outside. It is determined by the external as much as it is determined by the internal. Spinoza points out the two elements that define the body. The first is the intrinsic and extrinsic movements, any action taking place within or outside. Second comes the plane of effect; the internal effect and the external effect—wherever the body is situated, how the milieu affects it and how it interacts with it. Bodies will never be defined as exclusive, but their definitions are driven by their interactions with other bodies (Connolly 2001, 123–4).

Kari's life continues with a continuous want for a compassionate listener. The term compassionate listener becomes very important here because, throughout the novel, we find Kari searching for company, a person she can share her thoughts with. She finds one such person through her ad agency. Angel, her new boss, is a cancer patient awaiting her death. Kari develops a complex friendship with her. This relationship also brings in the idea of sexuality. They share a very intimate space; she usually visits Angel's house and they both talk their hearts out to each other. The deep conversations that take place in this house also highlight one of the pertinent questions the novel deals with—the question of existence and identity.

The term identity crisis was coined by theorist Erik Erikson (1968). He claimed that the "identity crisis" (11) is the main conflict faced by people in the era of chaos, that is, the modern era. According to him, an identity crisis is a time of intensive analysis and exploration of different ways of looking at oneself. He described identity as:

> ... a subjective sense as well as an observable quality of personal sameness and continuity, paired with some belief in the sameness and continuity of some shared world image. As a quality of unself-conscious living, this can be gloriously obvious in a young person who has found himself as he has found his communality. In him we see emerge a unique unification of what is irreversibly given – that is, body type and temperament, giftedness and vulnerability, infantile models and acquired ideals – with the open choices provided in available roles, occupational possibilities, values offered, mentors met, friendships made, and first sexual encounters (12).

Kari's graph is presented to the reader as that of a struggling identity throughout the novel—when she is questioned by her parents about Ruth, her new life in the city, new room, relationship with her new roommates, apathetic connection with her boss and continuous search for a space which she can call her own in this new world. The colourless frames of the novel illustrate the struggle of Kari.

> Like any other morning, we travel in silence. In this city, no one talks. Everyone guards their sanity against the grief of strangers. We see a dismembered body on the tracks, but after the first gasp, no one utters a word (Patil 2008, 42).

Patil's protagonist feels excluded by her community. She is unable to comprehend the desires of the expressionless passengers who are just two inches away from one another. She longs for strong companionship, friendship and a sense of closeness in all her relations. When she meets Alexa and her husband, Manuel, one day on her way to work, she feels a happy buzz in her heart after a long time. Interestingly, she compares this little buzz to the happiness she always felt with

Ruth. To her dismay, she never finds the road to Alexa's house again:

> It needs to be mentioned that when I looked for the road to Alexa and Manuel's house the next morning, it was not there. I have seen it since, once or twice, but I can never be entirely sure when I will find it next (Patil 2008, 46).

This interesting incident in Kari's isolated life represents her wanting happiness and the warmth of a close relationship, which is quite difficult to gain in the disjunct metropolitan city of Mumbai. Kari is happy when she hears that Fairy-tale Hair has appointed a replacement for Angel. She is thrilled about the idea of a romantic possibility with her new boss, Susan Lush,

> ...my heart is an expanse of green grass at the sight of the name. ... Can you see her the way I do? Susan, Lush against watermelon walls. Susan, Lush against Grecian blue or white. Susan, Lush and tan on a bone-white beach. Susan, Lush and succulent, all salt, all sun (Patil 2008, 64).

In the concluding part of the novel, we see Kari again atop a building, fighting the desire to jump off. But this time, she does not jump off. She imagines someone called "Pigeon Girl" (Patil 2008, 113) who jumps off, an alter ego for Kari's desire. Kari realises that she doesn't feel the urge to jump anymore; she wants to "step back, not step off" (115) and also that she still cares for Ruth, "I still love Ruthie more than anyone else in the world, but I won't be jumping off ledges for anyone anymore" (115). This is where Kari embraces herself just as she is and leaves Ruth smiling in a faraway city.

Conclusion

Amruta Patil's *Kari* problematises not only the issues of being a lesbian woman but also a woman who is divided between selves of selfhood, between the normative and the not-so-normative belief systems. She becomes a body without organs, somebody who has lost all meaning in being the organic entity that she is. Thus, on a close reading of the novel, one can discover how Patil's protagonist bears the burden of the social mores and isolates herself from her territory, her identity, her environment and even from herself. Society alienates her from her own consciousness. It debars her from her sanity. Not putting herself before others or everything else leads to the shelving of her identity. Deleuze, very succinctly, has pointed to the idea of construction. Every construction is prehuman. It is micropolitical and not macropolitical or metapolitical. Freedom, according to Deleuze, needs to be redefined and be refined in a sense where we understand that we get affected by forces that lie beyond our horizons. Freedom is the power to look inside and reaffirm the power that lies within and not outside. Meanings are essentially prehuman and such meanings cannot be or act like our transforming agents. Kari does not communicate her thoughts and keeps herself isolated. This leads to her fall or her suicide. Towards the end, we witness a subject who rises back from the stench to a more confident version of herself. It is only when she realises that external meanings cannot act like her transforming agents that we see a Kari who finally overcomes her amorphous identity and shuns away from the politics of perception. The perception here is not the window of the outer world; it is but the encounter with the desires of being and becoming.

Works Cited

Banerjee, Sarnath. 2004. *Corridor*. New Delhi: Penguin Books.

Butler, Judith. 2006. *Gender Trouble: Feminism and the Subversion of Identity*. New York; London: Routledge.

Connolly, William E. 2001. "Spinoza and Us." *Political Theory* 29 (4): 583–94. https://doi.org/10.1177/0090591701029004006.

Deleuze, Gilles, and Felix Gauttari. 1992. *Ethology: Spinoza and Us*. New York: Zone Books.

———. 2013. *A Thousand Plateaus: Capitalism and Schizophrenia*. London: Bloomsbury Academic.

Eisner, Will. 2008. *Comics and Sequential Art: Principles and Practices from the Legendary Cartoonist*. New York: W.W. Norton.

Erikson, Erik. 1968. *Identity Youth and Crisis*. New York: W. W. Norton.

Ghosh, Vishwajyoti. 2010. *Delhi Calm*. New Delhi: HarperCollins.

Griffiths, Morwenna. 1995. *Feminisms and the Self: The Web of Identity*. London: Routledge.

Hall, Donald E. 2003. *Reading Sexualities*. New York: Palgrave Macmillan.

Natarajan, Srividya and Anand. S. 2011. *Bhimayana: Experiences of Untouchability*. New Delhi: Navayana.

Patil, Amruta. 2008. *Kari*. India: Harper Collins.

Sartre, Jean-Paul. 2007. *Existentialism Is a Humanism*. Translated by Carol Macomber, Yale University Press.

Sedgwick, Eve Kosofsky. 1990. *Epistemology of the Closet*. Berkeley: University of California Press.

Sen, Orijit. 1994. *River of Stories*. New Delhi: Kalpavriksha.

2

Gender and Violence in Indian Graphic Narratives

Sandhya Nayak

Introduction

Indian graphic narratives have evolved with time. The Indian woman, who was portrayed as the subdued, beautiful woman with a perfect figure, the epitome of goodness and virtue, the hapless lover or the obedient wife, has undergone a radical change in the graphic narratives of India. To analyse the gradual change in the representation of women in the world of Indian graphic narratives, it is important to take into account the women protagonists of *Amar Chitra Katha*—the very first Indian comic series[1]. The series has published many comic books on the lives of historical and mythological female characters, like *Savitri* (Pai 1970), *Draupadi* (Chandrakant 1974a), *Padmini* (Sharma 1973), Sita in *Ramayana* (Pai 1971), *Urvashi* (Chandrakant 1974b) and others. Although it appears like a space for women has been created in the comic series, a closer analysis of the narratives will reveal that there is a rigid categorisation of the female characters. *Padmini* is the mythical story of a queen who committed *Jauhar*, a Rajput custom of self-immolation, along with many other women and children to protect themselves from sexual assault by foreign invaders. Sita, the female protagonist of the Sanskrit epic *Ramayana*, had to undergo an ordeal of purification through fire to prove her chastity to her husband. The plotline of *Savitri* upholds the strong will of a wife to save her husband from the God of death, Yama. In her efforts to bring back her husband from death, Savitri proposes to give up her own life as well. Savitri, Padmini and Sita are protagonists who are eulogised for their sole virtue of sacrificing their lives and their desires for their husbands. The sole identity of the women in this context lies in their role as dutiful wives, adhering to traditional gender norms in a patriarchal society. The different forms of violence, such as harassment of a widow in *Padmini*, Sita's trial by fire to prove chastity in *Ramayana* and the act of begging for a husband's life in *Savitri*, are presented as normative behaviour, while the supreme sacrifice made by the women in the larger interest of society is upheld as a model for future women.

The image of the virtuous Hindu woman, which initially appears in Sanskrit epics, was further described and developed through early Indian literary texts such as folk tales and children's literature. A deeply entrenched notion of the ideal woman in Indian society has thus been periodically reinforced in history. Moreover, when this good wife began to be illustrated in comic books, her body became the focal point of the narratives. The practice is particularly evident in the case of the *Amar Chitra Katha* comic, *Draupadi* (Chandrakant 1974a). Draupadi is a character from *The Mahabharata* and is one of the most iconic female characters of Hindu mythology as she became the dutiful wife of all the five Pandava princes to keep them united, following them in their exile. Nonetheless, Draupadi is not the demure, passive sufferer of patriarchy like Sita, Savitri or other glorified mythical women. She questions the imperial court and the king when she is disrobed and treated as an object of desire in the court by the Kauravas. Throughout the epic, Draupadi's narrative has created many spaces to raise the issues of gender inequality and objectification of women. Although she had submissively accepted her polyandrous fate, she later proves to be rebellious and fiery while voicing her opinions against the patriarchal symbolic order, as well as seeking revenge against her abusers. In the grand storyline of *The Mahabharata*, Draupadi is a woman who manifested the possibility to subvert gender power structures of the society—an aspect that was further developed in several literary texts by Indian writers[2].

Gender-based violence exists largely because of inequitable gender norms. It can affect people at different points in their lives, ranging from intimate partner violence and sexual coercion to abuse and child marriage. Each of these can have physical, sexual, or emotional dimensions. Using pictures to tell stories has been a crucial medium in the history of humankind. We have evolved from drawing on stone and papyrus onto paper and digital formats, but the impact of the image remains the same. Recent graphic narratives produced in India portray Indian women in sync with Draupadi of *The Mahabharata*, who questions authority and revolts against the perpetrators in order to get justice.

Gender-Based Violence

Gender-based violence is defined as physical, sexual, and psychological harm. Over the past few decades, gender-based violence has increasingly gained recognition as a serious problem for the attainment of equality, development and peace for women. The issue has become a subject of feminist intervention and a priority for women's organisations in various parts of the world. Gender-based violence is a global problem, but to better understand the patterns and causes of violence and, hence, eliminate them, the starting point must be to acknowledge the historical and socio-cultural factors at work in each specific context. The specific nature of gender-based violence in India is that other serious forms of behaviour may also be identified as acts of violence. These types of conduct include verbal abuse and coercion, the infliction of physical injuries, serious bodily harm and sexual abuse. Gender-based violence is a human rights violation and is an extreme manifestation of gender inequity, targeting women and girls because of their subordinate social status in society. In all of its manifestations, it can have serious implications for a woman's sexual and reproductive health.

The escalation of comics and graphic novels in India from the late twentieth century ushered in a new kind of visual narrative produced mainly by women. These works showcase ordinary women in society and highlight their everyday struggles. In relation to the previous era of graphic stories, predominantly brought out by ACK and sometimes circulated as educative posters, these contemporary comics are shaping a literary subculture. This is a new female literary tradition, resembling the one that Elaine Showalter quotes as an observer of human malady: "But those women who succeeded in an epic life of resonant action should not be consigned to the anonymity and obscurity that is the common destiny of womanhood. The lives of the unknown are redeemed and transfigured by the spirits and the shrines of the great. We need to pay them tribute" (Showalter 2001, 337).

With the arrival of female graphic novelists and graphic artists, such as Amruta Patil, Priya Kuriyan, Rachita Taneja, Aarthi Parthasarathy, Kaveri Gopalakrishnan, Mounica Tata and many others, the space for female narratives in comics has also opened up and the characters have a much more powerful presence than before. Showalter has emphasised perceiving the "female literary tradition" in its entirety, "within the framework of a larger society" where these women are "unified by values, conventions, experiences, and behaviours impinging on each individual" (Showalter 1977, 11). There has to be an understanding of the "collective identity" (Showalter 1977, 12), leading to the formation of a subversive literary movement where numerous female graphic artists and writers of different times, as well as diverse platforms, can merge into a stronger voice in the hegemonic culture of patriarchy.

Amruta Patil's first graphic novel, *Kari* (2008), Priya Kuriyan's collection of graphic stories, *Drawing the Line: Indian Women Fight Back* (2015), the interactive comic project of *Priya's Shakti* (Devineni and Menon 2014), Rachita Taneja's webcomics, *Sanitary Panels* (2014) and Mounica Tata's *Doodledrama* (2013) can be considered elements of this larger movement of self-expression and resistance against the patriarchal order of the society. All these works bring forth the everyday problems of an ordinary woman and raise the question of sexuality and gender. The female characters illustrated by women are removed from the objectifying position of the readers' powerful male gaze and, at the same time, through their narrative journeys, they evolve as sexual beings.

Patil's *Kari* situates her female protagonist against the heteronormative structure of society and documents the lived realities of a homosexual woman in a modern and progressive metropolitan city. Kari and Ruth, two women in love, attempt suicide for not being able to find acceptance in society, but they are "saved" (Patil 2008, 8) and gradually drift away from each other. As the story unfolds, Kari is never actually saved and questions her existence repeatedly. Through her own quest for identity, Kari's experiences, in turn, pose numerous challenges to the "smog city" (16). The gaze that has always been directed towards the female body in ACK comics, elevating the male-dominated society to a position of authority and power, now zooms in on the dominant culture itself. Kari observes the city very intently and meticulously as she traverses through its superficiality and narrow definitions of femininity and relationships. In one of her acts of gazing, she is accompanied by her art director, Lazarus, and a camera. The panel shows them looking at the metropolis and Kari reflects,

> Laz and I have been walking around the city at night, camera in hand, watching homeless people deep in slumber. They sleep on roadsides, under carts and benches, on platforms. Arms holding bodies, legs under legs, a defensive ball against the threats that whiz past at night. It is an appalling this, this watching (78).

It is almost the body image of the "grim urban life" (Patil 2008, 78) that the protagonist records and analyses. In another instance, Kari again employs the two Foucauldian[3] instruments of power, observation and gaze, but this time she is looking at her naked body in a mirror. Interestingly, the reader cannot see any mirror in the illustration and Kari is directly facing the readers as she states,

> It's not that I have a bad relationship with the mirror. On the contrary, I think mirrors are splendid, shiny things that make great collectibles, whether whole or in smashed bits. Problem is, I just don't know what they are trying to tell me. These things can be troubling. The girls outside the

door telling me to wear kohl, and here I am wondering why I amn't looking like Sean Penn today (60).

By exposing her uncovered body to the readers, Kari allows herself to be subjected to the examining gaze of society. The short hair, dark eyes and vexed expression of Kari reveal the various ways in which society wants to formulate an identity for her, by asking her to wear kohl or marry a man and negate her own existence as a homosexual woman where she has to face the question, "[a]re you, like a proper lesbian?" (Patil 2008, 79). Through her confrontation with the mirror/readers she, in Foucault's words, "unveils the disguised examining gaze of the society" (Foucault 1977, 184). This gaze aims to cure and discipline her. The examination combines the techniques of an observing hierarchy and those of a normalizing judgement. It is a normalizing gaze, a surveillance that makes it possible to qualify, classify and punish. It establishes over individuals a visibility through which one differentiates them and judges them. That is why, in all the mechanisms of discipline, the examination is highly ritualised. In it are combined the ceremony of power and the form of the experiment, the deployment of force and the establishment of truth. At the heart of the procedures of discipline, it manifests the subjection of those who are perceived as objects and the objectification of those who are subjected (184–5).

Indian visual culture has persistently sculpted an ideal female body through its paintings, graphic stories, advertisements and films. This body is fetishised and dehumanised to please a largely male audience. It has constantly been put under strict examinations and disciplining. Owing to the excessive glorification of the bodies of Sita, Draupadi, Shakuntala and other mythical women by the dominant culture, the new age comic illustrators needed to depict the varied types of female bodies which exist in the world. The identities of these women transcend beyond their bodies and, hence, even though their bodies are subjected to the examining and differentiating gaze of society, they do not lose their agency. In other words, Kari's unhesitant acknowledgement of her body and presenting it before her readers strengthen the collective identity of Indian women and propels their movement of self-assertion and expression further (Showalter 1977, 14).

Drawing The Line

Technology and the internet have introduced a Utopian space for women that is, to an extent, away from the gender power dynamics of society. While many early cyber feminists had championed this optimism regarding the digital sphere, in the later years, the internet failed to become a postgender space[4]. It is inflicted with multifarious issues of sexual violence, stalking and gender discrimination. However, for Indian female comic artists, cyberspace has laid bare a range of dynamic possibilities to present their narratives. One of them is the webcomic format. Aarthi Parthasarathy, Kaveri Gopalakrishnan, Mounica Tata and Rachita Taneja are among the several women who have stepped into the world of comics through social media and blogs. Although female illustrators and writers of India had first appeared in the printed culture of comics, the number grew rapidly only in the digital medium. These artists foregrounded tabooed subjects and polemic topics of menstruation, politics, sexual harassment, marital rapes and similar issues, which never feature in the mainstream cultural domain.

Drawing The Line: Indian Women Fight Back (2015), an anthology by Priya Kurian Larissa Bertonasco and Ludmilla Bartscht, brings out fourteen stories written by women under the big, colourful, ever-expanding umbrella of feminist visual art.

That's Not Fair by Harini Kannan focuses on a sassy female foetus that defies societal norms. The female foetus—South Indian and dark-complexioned—is given a voice, as "In India, being dark is certainly not an asset. In order to avoid dowry, women take countless measures to lighten their complexion. In this case even the unborn child is not spared" (Kuriyan, Bertonasco, and Bartscht 2015, 8) The narrative is a commentary on skin tone prejudice and the resultant pressure on women with dark skin colour. The colour of the unborn foetus is pre-determined and beyond the colour of its mother, but that does not stop the elders from attempting to lighten its complexion in instances of dark humour. The practice of exclusion and discrimination based on a woman's skin tone is a deep-rooted problematic practice often perpetrated by women as much as men and has not received the attention it deserves. This points out in particular to women of South India who are doubly oppressed in this regard.

The Photo, is the story of a girl, Bena, who is reluctant to get married. The story is based on the writer/illustrator Reshu Singh's personal observation. She feels that in India, once girls reach a certain age, anxiety starts to build within Indian households. It is assumed that girls attain marriageable age. With more and more women choosing to get married late, it is a sign that they are acknowledging their lives and freedom. Women do not desire to slave in the kitchens all their lives. With women getting more educated and taking up good careers, marriage is not a priority for modern women. They have more autonomy and more choices to focus on other areas of their lives. Bena is critical of her family as she says, "My name is Bena. My family can't wait to marry me off and party hard at my wedding" (Kuriyan, Bertonasco, and Bartscht 2015, 23). *The Photo* uses Bena to portray the modern Indian girl who wishes to take control of her life by choosing to not get married purely for the sake of her family.

An Ideal Girl by Soumya Menon is a graphic narrative that attempts to turn things around through an exploration of some of the preset notions of the ideal girl. The writer wants the Ideal Girl to tell her own story, one in which she is set free. Despite India's reputation for respecting women to the extent of treating women as Goddesses, history tells us that women were ill-treated or neglected in various spheres of life across religions, regions and communities. Women are seen as nurturers and providers, while men are seen as financial providers. Right from childhood, girls inherit their mother's domestic chores and adopt stereotypical gender roles. Low self-esteem and self-worth are common. *The Ideal Girl* is synonymous with any girl in Indian households who has to play second fiddle to her brother and sacrifice all her desires while her brother gets to do what he wants. "They got her a bicycle so that she could get back home sooner. Instead, she cycled further and further away. She decided she had had quite enough of being the Ideal Girl" (Kuriyan, Bertonasco, and Bartscht 2015, 42). Finally, the Ideal Girl gets sick and tired of being undermined and decides to rebel.

The Prey by Neelima P. Aryan is based on a Malayalam story *Pennezhuttu* written by the writer, Prasanna Aryan 'Prayan'. In this story, the male gaze of a lecherous man is compared to that of a vulture. The protagonist of the story is a schoolgirl who captures the vulture in a rat trap, subverting the male gaze. The male gaze, according to feminist theory, is the act of showing women and the world from a masculine, heterosexual perspective in the visual arts and literature, which presents and represents women as sexual objects for the pleasure of the heterosexual male observer. The schoolgirl in *The Prey* chooses to not tell her mother about the lecherous man but traps the vulture, signifying her empowered mindset.

The Poet, Sharmila by Ita Mehrothra is about a close encounter she had with the Manipuri activist Irom Sharmila when she went all the way to Imphal to meet her at the hospital ward of Imphal Central Jail. Irom was on a fast to protest violence against women in Manipur, largely brought about by the strong presence of the military, who raped and looted at will with the protection of the Armed Forces Special Powers Act. Until quite recently, states took little action to combat violence against women (VAW), a comprehensive concept encompassing diverse phenomena, including rape, intimate partner violence, trafficking, honour killings and female genital mutilation. In fact, most states endorsed many types of violence, for example, through laws stating that sex was a marital obligation, that rapists could escape charges by marrying victims, that parents could marry off their girl children, or that men who murdered adulterous wives were merely defending honour. The diverse phenomena that we today call VAW was hardly recognised as a crime, let alone as a fundamental question of human rights (Htun 2020, 144).

"Rape or sexual abuse, when committed by a stranger, is often reported by the victim, and she is far more likely to be treated sympathetically. Sexual abuse within the family is far less reported, and a victim of incest is rarely heard and rarely gets justice" (Kuriyan, Bertonasco, and Bartscht 2015, 110) says Hemavathy Guha, the writer of the tenth graphic story in the anthology, *Asha, Now*, which brings out the trauma faced by Asha, who has to suffer in silence the repeated attempts by her brother to outrage her modesty, is not able to speak up and finally decides to stay in a women's hostel. She gets married but is hounded by the memories of her childhood in her dreams. She cannot completely get over the trauma and in addition, she feels she must protect her daughter from her uncle.

Broken Lines by Vidhyun Sabhaney is a critique of how the deluge of rape reportage has made voyeurs out of us. This story was triggered off by the media deluge that followed the gang rape of a medical student in New Delhi in 2012. Several images in the graphic narrative bear a striking resemblance to the punishment described in the *Manusmriti*, both in their didactic tone and violent nature. They range from genital mutilation by rubbing against a khejoor tree for committing adultery to having one's tongue pierced by sharp tongs for eating an offering meant for the Gods (Kuriyan, Bertonasco, and Bartscht 2015, 135).

Kaveri Gopalakrishnan in *Basic Space* seeks answers to a simple question: "What lines do you draw as a woman?" from different women belonging to different parts of society. It is a hilarious compilation of various responses that are at once comic and profound. While a woman uses pins as a weapon: "Just keep a few pins [in Chennai Buses]. My mother has been doing so for years" (Kuriyan, Bertonasco, and Bartscht 2015, 112), a young college girl says, "When I'm in that Bombay local train, my God, I'm like Goonda" (113). But between the lines, one knows that women are often stereotyped and are expected to conduct themselves in a certain way. The story also tells the readers candidly what women desire to do if there was complete freedom given to them.

Conclusion

From crassly objectifying female bodies to encouraging women to speak up, Indian graphic narratives have come a long way since their beginnings. They have not only expanded the space for female characters but also opened up the scope for female writers and illustrators. As a contemporary medium of popular culture, they have been able to impact gender representations in powerful ways. Comics and cartoons, in fact, have a history of offering critical commentary on significant political issues. While the earlier comics scene was dominated by male writers, digital graphic narratives are flooded with female writers. Consequently, the modern Indian superheroines are not coy, sacrificial and dutiful wives of the Vedic age. They are constantly putting up a fight against patriarchy, gender stereotyping, gender discrimination and violence against women as well as against their real-life abusers. While printed comics did address female sexuality and the female existential crises, the digital era has ushered in the issues of women's rights, stigmatisations, uncomfortable subjects and insurgence. In graphic novels, specifically, the visual medium enables the illustration of unvoiced thoughts through devices such as thought balloons, where the audience "sees" the mental/emotional state that would be otherwise suppressed. The form thus ensures a "visual grammar" that perhaps is made possible through the illustrative nature of the form, a feature not available in other written narratives (Nayar 2017, 232). There are an increasing number of women from rural and urban places who are participating in this culture of resistance and this movement of collective identity. They are achieving gender subversion by creating comics or even by sharing them on social media or talking about them in both personal and public spaces. Indian comics, therefore, manifest a huge prospect where they can evolve into a platform for women to speak up and for raising issues regarding gender justice. The transformation of gender roles and the redefinition of the heroine in Indian graphic narratives have been paralleled by a corresponding shift in authorship, signalling an exercise of agency by the woman author, who is often also the narrator of the autobiographical stories.

Endnotes

1. *Amar Chitra Katha* is an Indian publisher of comics and graphic novels founded in 1967 by Ananth Pai. Will be referred to as ACK in the rest of the chapter.

2. Writers such as Chitra Banerjee Divakaruni and Ira Mukhoty, for instance.
3. Michael Foucault in *The History of Sexuality* Volume one (1978).
4. postgender is a term that means moving beyond gender identities.

Works Cited

Allen, Amy. 2002. "Power, Subjectivity, and Agency: Between Arendt and Foucault."

International Journal of Philosophical Studies. vol. 10 no. 2, pp. 131–149. DOI: 10.1080/09672550210121432

Chandra, Nandini. 2010. "The *Amar Chitra Katha* Shakuntala: Pin-Up or Role Model?" *South Asia Multidisciplinary Academic Journal*, no. 4 (December). https://doi.org/10.4000/samaj.3050.

Chandrakant, Kamala. 1974a. *Draupadi*. Vol 72. Amar Chitra Katha Pvt Ltd.

———. 1974b. *Urvashi*. Vol. 59. Amar Chitra Katha Pvt Ltd.

Devineni, Ram, and Vikas K. Menon. 2014. *Priya's Shakti*. Rattapallax.

Flood, Alison. 2018. "Indian Comic Creates Female Superhero to Tackle Rape." *The Guardian*, February 22, 2018. https://www.theguardian.com/books/2014/dec/18/india-comic-superhero-tackle-rape-women-priyas-shakti-parvati.

Foucault, Michel. 1977. *Discipline And Punish: The Birth of The Prison*. Vintage Books.

Foucault, Michel. 1978. *The History of Sexuality* Vol. 1.

Htun, Mala, and Francesca R. Jensenius. 2020. "Fighting Violence Against Women: Laws, Norms & Challenges Ahead." *Daedalus* 149 (1): 144–59. https://doi.org/10.1162/daed_a_01779.

Kuriyan, Priya et al. (eds.). 2016. *Drawing the Line: Indian Women Fight Back*. New Delhi: Zubaan.

Madrid, Mike. 2009. *The Supergirls: Fashion, Feminism, Fantasy, and the History of Comic Book Heroines*. Exterminating Angel Press. http://ci.nii.ac.jp/ncid/BB0897734X.

Nayar, Pramod K. 2017. "Editor's Introduction: Gender and the Graphic." *Indian Journal of Gender Studies* 24 (2): 231–35. https://doi.org/10.1177/0971521517697882.

Nayek, Debanjana. 2020. "From Shakuntala to Sanitary Panels: Women in Indian Graphic Narratives." *FeministEncounters* 4 (1). https://doi.org/10.20897/femenc/7919.

Pai, Anant. 1970. *Savitri*. Vol. 14. Amar Chitra Katha Pvt Ltd.

Pai, Anant. 1971. *Valmiki's Ramayana*. Amar Chitra Katha Pvt Ltd.

Patil, Amruta. 2008. *Kari*. Harper Collins.

Sharma, Yagya. 1973. *Padmini*. Vol. 44. Amar Chitra Katha Pvt Ltd.

Showalter, Elaine. 1977. *A Literature of Their Own: British Women Novelists from Bronte to Lessing*. Princeton University Press.

Showalter, Elaine. 2001. *Inventing Herself: Claiming a Feminist Intellectual Heritage*. http://ci.nii.ac.jp/ncid/BA52264734.

3

The Impact of Social Paradigms and its Resonance on the Characters of Sarnath Banerjee's *Corridor*

Smita Dabi

Introduction

Though there is indeed a transformation when one traces the growth of India in all possible contexts, the one stagnant phenomenon that can be termed as the social behavioural issue, wherein one can observe the age-old practices, belief systems and notions still being observed. These paradigms or preconceived notions of society go a long way in determining the behavioural patterns of individuals. Individuals constituting society act according to the expectations of the milieu. Thus, one can say that it is a vicious cycle wherein the individual, being a part of the society, acts according to their expectations, in turn supporting the beliefs hitherto held and augmenting its practice in the future. The purpose of this chapter is to explore the influence of societal coercions on the individual persona, goading them indirectly into behaving according to a certain set pattern acceptable to society. The impact of this societal coercion on the individual's life and individuality will be explored via the characters of the graphic novel *Corridor* (2004) by Sarnath Banerjee. Luniewska (2019), in her article *New Genres And Forms Of Storytelling In India*, speaks about the significance of the visual aspect of the technique of literary narration. The author further talks about the art of storytelling through images and how contemporary issues are reflected in these narratives.

Srinivasan (2016) speaks of the artistic creations of Sarnath Banerjee as works trailing the growth of India in general and its minuscule individuals into a modern contemporary world.

Social Paradigms

According to Dunn (2021), paradigms are belief systems that can lead to the development of theories. She goes on to explain in detail the concept of conflict paradigms in the same article titled *The Three Sociological Paradigms and Perspectives*. According to this theory, the process of socialisation is coercive, goading everyone to accept the societal norms and values hitherto laid down and followed by the working class, which is in the majority. Burrell and Morgan (1979) contend whether humans can exercise free will or are conditioned solely by their surroundings. Burrell and Morgan (1979), in their book *Sociological Paradigms and Organisational Analysis*, speak of the true nature of knowledge to be passed on from one individual to another, whether the reality is an external feature or the product of one's mind or consciousness. The behaviour of an individual may be affected by this reality, which can be knowledge that is passed on or something inferred by an individual. Whatever that may be, the result can be a psychological conflict, as mirrored in the characters of *Corridor*.

Sarnath Banerjee's novels reflect modern reality, which can be seen in his graphic novel *Corridor*. The novel can be interpreted as an assemblage of the individual stories of four different and interesting characters, including the journey of their existence. The story indeed has a beautiful and picturesque beginning, with the readers being taken on a visual tour of the corridors of Connaught Place. At the very onset, one comes across one of the major protagonists of the novel, the obsessive collector Brighu, roaming the corridors of Delhi. There is a hint of reflection and self-realisation right at the beginning when he says, "let's face it, I can get quite obsessive sometimes" (Banerjee 2004, 4). The loneliness of urban life is depicted through the words of Brighu, when he says that there were times he spent entire afternoons looking at his toes and speaking to a lizard whom he had named Gustav. The impossible search is highlighted when

Brighu mentions that, for him, it always involves seeking the impossible. It is the thrill of the search that keeps him energised with a sense of purpose. The moment the investigation is complete, he is deflated and dies within. It is his plethora of collections that comforts him. It is his inner circle of sanctity and comfort that he does not wish to leave. Hence, he is reluctant to utilise the collections he so painstakingly makes, revealing the underlying fear and insecurity of human nature. The ridiculing of the everyday banter and the simplistic assumptions of the naïve is also brought forth through the character of Brighu, who somehow realises the depths of his problems. As a result, he ridicules the simplistic assumptions made by his cousin. He is inadvertently drawn to Kali yet does not wish to make the final commitment. The search for perfection, another paradigm of a perfect society, continues for him till the end. It appears as if he does not want the paradigms of perfectionism to be shattered, hence the reluctance to use the objects attained after an incredulous search or an unwillingness to accept a life partner. He is a part of society yet rebels by looking for the wholeness he feels he lacks. A society with its definite parameters forces him to look inward and contemplate. He is defined by society yet is on a search of his own. As his search continues, the paradigms slightly appear to shift for him, but not completely. However, he appears to be a tad wiser at the end, as one can see him musing on the coincidences of life, bringing individuals together by cosmic interventions.

Jehangir Rangoonwalla, "the Cyrus of second-hand books" (Banerjee 2004, 14), is another significant character in the novel. He considers his bookstore to be the centre of his universe and appears to be a self-satisfied individual dispensing unsolicited advice to others. He appears to be wise, yet a simpleton at heart who is satisfied with his present and is not seeking to accomplish more. He is shown reminiscing about his younger days when he had been swapping jobs and seeking to find the perfection that appeared to be an illusion. Finally, the paradigms shift for him, and in a fraction of a second, he unearths the answer to his search in a lift. The answer is to chew one's food properly, which is symbolic of savouring what one has at present rather than seeking the unknown, the mirage. The rebel in him helps him ponder over the paradigms and restrictions forcing him to seek the perfect life, which ultimately turns out to be a mirage. Introspection aids him in self-exploration, inner peace and tranquillity, not bound by the perceptions of a perfectionist society. Hence, his search ends and he is shown contented dispensing secondhand books, tea and advice.

The third significant character of the novel is Prof. Murthy, who also happens to be the most interesting one. His life is an oxymoron, as he is fond of poetry, specifically John Keats, the poet of nature and its beauty, signifying all that is beautiful in life, yet he deals with death every day. Prof. Murthy, the head of the Department of Jurisprudence and Forensic Sciences, loves his profession, which is to perform autopsies every evening. Hence, his life revolves around his two passions, the beauty of life and the end of that beautiful life, death. He gets stoned to cope with the stench of death yet is secretly addicted to it. Marijuana and poetry become his escape from his reality as well as his addictions. Prof. Murthy cannot leave his profession, not even for the sake of the love he has for his small daughter. The smell of death seems to have seeped into his soul, yet he is attracted to the beauty of life as well. Herein lies the predicament of his existence—the stench of death and the beauty of life. However, the paradigms shift when he discovers a perfume that would finally drive away the smell of death and bring his daughter closer to him. The answer is not just the perfume itself. It might be related to his attitude towards life and the perfume might be a catalyst for the same. The perfume might also represent a shift in the way he perceives himself through the eyes of societal parameters. No matter how hard one tries, the attachment that one has to their social environment can also lead to a perennial state of affliction unless one decides to make a significant change in one's perspective.

The paradoxes of life are varied, and one such paradox is evident in the life of Digital, another important character of this novel who is plagued by the ideologies of Karl Marx. He is torn between the desire to satisfy the demands of his would-be father-in-law and his desire to work for the upliftment of the underprivileged. His predicament is not resolved till the end as he is torn between the desire to fulfil what society expects of him and the innate longing to pursue what his heart desires, pushing him to live in a world of imagination. The need to prove one's worth creates disharmony in any relationship and within oneself, as is evident in Digital Dutta. He is perplexed by the paradigms of society, which need one to have wealth and an overseas job to prove their validation of existence, causing disharmony. Yet, Digital beating the goons somehow verifies his existence, lending a harmonious air to his relationship with Dolly, his girlfriend, again proving the preconceived social norms of masculinity. Yet for him, the search and conflict within him continues and the paradigms of his personal life wait for the conclusive shift.

The character of Angrez Bosch is the epitome of the search for the futile. He appears to be on an endless search, just like the other characters, yet his search finally leads him to follow what society deems fit for a perfect life. Initially, he appears to be a rebel, going inwards on a search for the seemingly unattainable. However, his search culminates at the threshold of the very paradigms he was making an endeavour to escape from, thus making him a part of the perfect illusionistic life that society envisages for its individuals.

Finally, the enigmatic yet universally accepted character of Shintu has been described in detail by the author. The graphics may be hilarious at times, but they appear to portray the paradigms of our society. The rules and norms of a good boy are depicted by the bold graphics of the good boy rules that one observes in old moralistic textbooks. The dilemma of the unsatisfied, insecure individual is brought forth through this character. Shintu is a classic example of the insecure urban human, not certain of his prowess and seeking validation at every level. He is the epitome of the disillusioned individual, conditioned by society's parameters and paradigms, seeking to satisfy his deepest desire for a belief in himself and his capabilities.

Paradoxes of Life

The *Corridor* is a satire on the paradoxes of life. It is Banrejee's humorous take on the paradigms of individual and societal existence. The references such as "Chengiz Khan" (Banerjee 2004, 3) for the protagonist Brighu symbolising his search in life, the warrior in him and also that of "Ibn Batuta" (106), the famous traveller, all tend to subtly denote his chief characteristics. The collection, the obsessive search, the breakup with Kali—all tend to denote something profound. The chewing of the food by Jehangir Rangoonealla and its implicit meaning; the paradox of Dr. Murthy's life represented by the beauty of poetry and death points to the irony of life. Finally, the dilemma of Digital Dutta and the insecurity of Shintu are laid bare before the readers. Shintu is still shown searching for a means of enhancing his sexual prowess and being validated and accepted by society.

The entire novel has innumerable aspects of wit, humour and satire. Jehangir coming to terms with the essence of life in a few split seconds in the lift, the maid going bald after using the oil meant for Shintu, and Shintu, in turn, smelling the hair oil all are certain examples of the wit, humour and satire employed by the author. These instances aim at the elucidation of the shallowness and hypocrisy of the society that we inhabit.

One gets the impression of over-dramatisation in this novel. It also appears to be disjointed at times; for instance, the sudden shift in the narrative gives the impression of a film rather than a novel. The shift from a colourful graphic detail to a black-and-white one also tends to highlight the same. Moreover, the overtly dramatic graphics tend to overemphasise certain facts and appear to be a bit theatrical, emphasising the overall effect of a dream-like quality of the almost perfect existence that the characters would like to live.

The Sociological Theories Revealing the Social Impact on Individuals

According to Lanning (2021), the relationship and attachment that one has with others significantly affect the personality of the individual. Cooley (1902) contended that individuals tend to perceive themselves according to the perception of society, terming it as "the looking glass self" (179–185). According to Mund, Jeronimus and Neyer (2018), in their book chapter, *Personality and Social Relationships: As Thick as Thieves*, social relationships are an integral part of an individual's life and being accepted socially is crucial to their sense of well-being. Thus, society, with or without its parameters of acceptance, is extremely vital to an individual's existence.

The symbolic interaction theory focuses on the interaction between individuals in society, highlighting the interpretation of these actions, where perspectives matter a great deal (Aksan et al. 2009). It also proposes that an individual's perspective is formed by the interactions that they have with their family and close associates. Thus, these perspectives are significant in the way one perceives oneself. Hence, one can say that societal interactions eventually give shape to the way we perceive ourselves. Herein comes the notable effects of the societal paradigms and their resonance felt in the lives of individuals. One can observe the effect of these interactions in the lives of all the characters, be it Brighu with his endless futile search for perfection or Digital Dutta and Shintu searching for an elusive proof of masculinity. The author exposes the hypocrisy of social interactions through the conversations between the fellow inhabitants of a shallow, hypocritical society, where everyone is most extraordinary.

Gender performativity theory, according to Judith Butler (1990), speaks about gender as performances. One performs according to the perceptions of society, envisaging a certain role for each gender, thus creating categories in which individuals have to fit themselves (Morgenroth and Ryan 2018). Befitting examples of this theory are exemplified in the characterisation of almost all characters. They seek to validate their acceptance as courageous male figures, as portrayed through the valiant fighter saving his lady love from disgrace or valiantly trying to reinforce their masculinity in terms of their sexual prowess, as seen in Shintu's case.

Cherry (2020), in the article titled *Freud's Id, Ego and Superego*, contends that an individual's personality is shaped in stages. There is a certain balance and interconnectedness between an individual's id, ego and superego that finally results in the shaping of an individual's personality. The development of an individual's ego and superego helps in subverting the basic urges of the Id, to make them act in a realistic and socially acceptable manner. The psychological aspect deals with the psychoanalysis of characters, which delves into the deep recesses of one's psyche to find the answers to one's psychological conflicts. The numerous conflicts, as evident in the characters, are almost always influenced by the societal parameters of right and wrong. One glaring example of this conflict is when Brighu decides to speak the truth to his beloved at the end of the novel, culminating at the end of their relationship. Nothing is perfect in this illusionary world, where doing the supposedly right thing does not always work out. The soul searching and the acceptance are also evident in most of the characters, especially Brighu and Jehangir Rangoonwalla, who appear to know themselves. However, the turmoil for Brighu especially continues.

Conclusion

Sarnath Banerjee's graphic novel *Corridor* is an interesting portrayal of the quandary of human life. It is a satire on the paradigms of urban society, with its need for the individual's ratification of certain standard rules and norms to feel accepted and validated. The search for this acceptance, validation, contentment and finally peace is endless. For some, it comes to a fruitful culmination, for instance, the bookseller Jehangir Rangoonwalla and Angrez Bosch, who, after immeasurable soul searching and experiments, decide to go back to their native place and practice web designing. For others like Brighu, Shintu and Digital Dutta, the search continues, as the paradigms that shape them and appear to be monitoring their lives refuse to be altered or shifted. The satisfaction and contentment that finally comes to Jehangir and Dr. Murthy are elusive for these characters. Finally, the author also hints at the fact we are all the same, conditioned by the same factors and looking for the same essentialities of life. The phrase uttered by the bookseller stays with the reader till the end: "People are like onions, baba they have layers and layers but who will know? Who has time?" (Banerjee 2004, 111) There are layers of superficial existence to be peeled off and unearthed. The existential dilemma is ubiquitous and unavoidable.

Works Cited

Aksan, Nilgun, Buket Kisac, Mustafa Aydin, and Sezin Eren Demirbuken. 2009. "Symbolic Interaction Theory." *Procedia - Social and Behavioral Sciences* 1 (1): 902–4. https://doi.org/10.1016/j.sbspro.2009.01.160.

Banerjee, Sarnath. 2004. *Corridor*. Penguin Books India.

Burrell, Gibson, and Gareth Morgan. 1979. *Sociological Paradigms and Organisational Analysis*. Athenaeum Press Ltd.

Butler, Judith. 1990. *Gender Trouble*. Routledge.

Cherry, Kendra. 2020. "Id, Ego, and Superego: Freud's Elements of Personality." *Verywell Mind*, November. https://www.verywellmind.com/the-id-ego-and-superego-2795951.

Cooley, Charles Horton. 2017. *Human Nature and the Social Order. Routledge EBooks*. https://doi.org/10.4324/9780203789513.

Dunn, Ruth. 2021. "8.1: The Three Sociological Paradigms and Perspectives." *Social Sci LibreTexts*, February. socialsci.libretexts.org/Bookshelves/Sociology/Cultural_Sociology_and_Social_Problems/Minority_Studies_(Dunn)/08%3A_The_Three_Sociological_Paradigms/8.01%3A_The_Three_Sociological_Paradigms_and_Perspectives.

Lanning, Kevin. 2017. "What Is the Relationship Between 'Personality' and 'Social' Psychologies? Network, Community, and Whole Text Analyses of The Structure of Contemporary Scholarship." *Collabra* 3 (March): 1–15. https://doi.org/10.1525/collabra.70.

Junik Łuniewska, Kamila. 2019. "Towards the Visual. New Genres and Forms of Storytelling in India." *Politeja*, no. 59: 149–60.

Morgenroth, Thekla, and Michelle K. Ryan. 2018. "Gender Trouble in Social Psychology: How Can Butler's Work Inform Experimental Social Psychologists' Conceptualization of Gender?" *Frontiers in Psychology* 9 (July): 1–1320. https://doi.org/10.3389/fpsyg.2018.01320.

Mund, Marcus, Bertus F. Jeronimus, and Franz J. Neyer. 2018. "Personality and Social Relationships." In *Elsevier EBooks*, 1–47. https://doi.org/10.1016/b978-0-12-805300-3.00009-8.

Srinivasan, Ragini Tharoor. 2016. "A Graphic Novelist Captures the Paradoxes of Living in the 'New India.'" *The New Yorker*, August 13, 2016. https://www.newyorker.com/books/page-turner/a-graphic-novelist-captures-the-paradoxes-of-living-in-the-new-india.

4

Cityscapes and Real-Imagined Spatiality: Locating Topophrenia in Amruta Patil's *Kari*

Nidhi Sharma

Yi-Fu Tuan (1977) harped on the emotive connect between the human and the place. How spaces (wide and open vast geographies) can become demarcated as places depend upon human interest, which is based on physical interaction, contact with the land affiliation/affinity towards homely, friendly places and objects of gaze that may impact humans' pleasure, howsoever fleeting it be. *Kari* (2008) provides an exploratory potential in the field of spatiality in several ways. Kari, a young independent girl who has come to the city to work in an ad agency, finds the "thought of home" oppressive (Patil 2008, 10). She finds the geography of the urban space undergoing a massive transformation after her beloved Ruth flees the city forever. "A city alters when a person leaves. It drops drawbridges, grows new roads, looks hairy at dusk" (14). What rendered meaning to the cityscape, including the roads and the bridges, was the presence of Ruth. Virginia Woolf (1997) in her essay on *Literary Geography* uses two terms to describe how readers can be placed within categories of "pilgrims from sentiment" and others as "scientific pilgrims" depending upon how and in what ways they connect with the places of the texts (158). The former term derives the spatial significance from the emotive response felt by the readers, as in the case of Kari, where her topophilia was largely shaped by Ruth's friendship and love. Kari's superlative declaration of love for Ruth comes right in the opening of the novel, "I am the one who loved her most in the world" (5). Strangely after attempting suicide, she rushes to her workplace, the ad agency cubicle, to help her cling to her sanity (11). At this time, Kari is resorting to the practice of cognitive mapping to surmount the anxiety associated with the place. This is a crucial juncture in her life and Kari's bewilderment is explicit in the description of structures like "coils" and "snakes" around her (8). It is that time when it is a must for the titular protagonist to figure out any signpost or point of reference that can help her surmount the "transcendental homelessness" (Lukacs 1971, 41) experienced in the story.

Why do we think of mapping in a graphic text like *Kari*? What purpose does it achieve? Literary cartography in novels helps the readers form mental maps of places and orient their own connections to the places, even in the absence of pictures. Amruta Patil's debut novel *Kari* depicts a freewheeling style, as she would like to call it. Comics and graphic novels generally adhere to patterns of panels, boxes and visual text features. What fascinatingly connects the graphic world with the mapping exercise is the possibility of projecting an alternate world.

Schwarz (2002) also points out the feature of alterity in the graphic genre in creating a parallel view of culture and life in "accessible ways" for the readers (264). The novel also subtly tells the story of Kari, whose queerness is not the overarching definition of her personality but an incidental feature of her being. As an intriguing storyteller, Patil carefully prepares her story for the audience, who seems to have grown up in the medium of *Amar Chitra Katha* and other mythological stories in this genre. What came out as a major milestone for the literary tradition of the graphic genre was a debut milestone for her. As her first work, Patil as an artist was also working out the fluidity of her creativity in new ways. Quite surprisingly the genre still battles against the low-brow perception bias but managed to win the Shakti Bhakt Award even in the pre-pride days. The writer as well as Kari set out together in their quests, sharing the spirit of their androgynous selves. Patil calls Kari "an androgynous version of myself" and "close to my skin"

(Junoon - A Stage for Theatre 2019). Patil's attempt to convey the difference in sexuality came out of her desire not to fit in with the hegemonic authoritative regime of gender norms. Hence, she experiments with gutters and choice of colours, like the free mapping where the scale can vary depending upon what are the focal points of emphasis and what places and ideas can be omitted or reduced.

The juxtaposition of words and texts in the novel makes the mapping layered and celebratory. But the presence of illustrations is not a prerequisite for the mapping exercise. Illustrations in *Kari* do not diminish word primacy because pictures are placed between voice overs. Reading the text to locate features of topophrenia must find its beginning points in the varied ways of seeing the vast array of the unrepresentable reality and dark texture of it, conveyed through sewage, toxicity and smog. These symbols are visually articulated in the cityscapes but still offer readers the real-imagined spaces produced in the textual readings as epistemological devices to understand the present and imagine a different space for the future.

Metropolitan spaces have mobile icons of reality in the constellation web of complex relations of power and knowledge between its elements. Kari, therefore, relies upon her experience of walking in the city to make sense of everyday practices of life. Instances such as idol immersion, her own passage through the gutter, choking smog, the playfulness of kittens on the way and so forth demonstrate several ways of engaging with the spatial contours of the city. Henri Lefebvre's production of space can be directly linked to Kari's discovery of new roads, which she says cannot be walked upon twice. In the mode of magic realism, she seems to walk into new zones and back to the known coordinates of her home or office. The real-imagined liminalities are part of her flaneur act. "Everyday I wander into strange backyards and junk heaps" (Patil 2008, 14) and discover something swinging between the topophilic and topohobic.

The love of a place is called topophilia. While home is the first place associated with topophilic aesthetics, here in the novel, it is far away from the sunny view of a place, nowhere embedded in the warmth and comfort of the homey and the familiar. However, the professional space allows her to reconcile conflict with survival adaptability, which she calls "paging inner fox" (Patil 2008, 11). Kari offers a profound and deeply layered understanding of places. Humans relate to their material environment with affective ties, for instance, the phone booth gives immensity to the emotion experienced by Kari as a daughter, but her monosyllabic responses of one word as short phrases limit the topophilia. Raymond Williams (1973), the British Marxist and cultural theorist in *The Country and The City*, spoke of "structures of feeling" (Tally 2013, 86). The term carried human responses to places and spaces in the way individuals add meanings to the places through an actively lived and felt experience. Hence, the phone booth is not essentially a place with singular topophilia, but also topophobia since Kari must watch her words with her mother, who is also part of the hegemonic structures of society that normalise heterosexuality and pass it on as the natural norm.

The union of topophilia and topophobia constitutes a structure of tension and interlocking responses. Hence, the novel calls our attention to the inclusive condition of topophrenia where both the topophilic and topophobic tendencies express themselves in simultaneity.

This chapter purports to locate topophrenia in the novel *Kari*. So, what is topophrenia? In what ways does the tour of the text unravel the topophrenic sensibilities? Robert Tally's book *Topophrenia: Place, Narrative and the Spatial Imagination* (2018) defines the titular term as a condition of simultaneity that incorporates place consciousness coupled with a sense of uncanniness. The term is loaded with associations of Freud's (1930) *Unbehagen in der Kultur* (*Civilisation and its Discontents*) and existential perplexities expressed by Martin Heidegger and Jean Paul Sartre.

The angle of real-imagined spatiality is an inevitable accompanying feature of literary cartographic reading. Edward Soja in his book *Thirdspace* (1996) uses the terms real and imagined to problematise the idea of representation. Since a literary cartographic reading sees the writer as a mapmaker undertaking the task of surveying the territories, in the process, the novel becomes a platform that presents places, either within the realm of imaginary geographies or places with certain referential coordinates. This leads the readers to reconfigure the coordinates of where we live and therefore engage in various ways of seeing. In a graphic text like *Kari*, the interplay of words and pictures opens up vivid frames of reference because, at some points, pictures take over words, as shown in the section on Snow Globe when Kari visits Angel and shows her the tattoo on her back. The picture not only shows the wings, like that of an angel, but also builds up the story of Kari as a boatman. Those who are familiar with Patil's style would know that the themes of death and resurrection are imaginatively articulated in her graphics. This liminality of the picture and the meaning it generates is a necessity for negotiating the realms of the real imminent death of Angel due to cancer and imagined alternative space (hope for an afterlife). The reference is connected to Charon, who typically labours to ferry souls across the Styx. Styx, like the sewage of *Kari*, is poisonous. As the myth goes, if anyone touches the black waters of the river, it would be fatal. But Kari navigates and plays her role like the Boatman of Hades. This is an interesting take on the role of Kari, who is also a queer protagonist. In this creative act of presentation, Kari's sexuality, however, does not limit her role of an angel who can possibly create possibilities of seeing life in otherworldly territories. If Kari's body sketches the wings of a large bird projecting hope for an alternate world, it is true that the novel then is not only a way to represent spaces but also produces spaces. As Edward Said discussed in the second chapter of *Orientalism* (1978) titled 'Imaginative Geography and Its Representations: *Orientalizing the Oriental*', space is not just a container but also holds the promise of actively and effectively shaping the world (49).

With this, *Kari* seems to have made its point; not declaratively coming out like a political book on queer rights but integrating a story through pictures and words, blurring lines between real and imaginary. It aims to represent a queer protagonist who does not so far belong to the societal order, yet her affinity to reach out to people in distress is a standout feature. She is not only aware of her hunger but through ways of seeing, she identifies with the hunger of others too. The essence of Kari's queerness is captured fleetingly in a mobile world and with carefully trodden steps. This was the time when queer themes addressed through a graphic novel were shaping the comic medium with a refined literary taste. The adult themes woven into the story of a young queer heroine were also unprecedented for bringing out their challenges in India, particularly in the urban city of the country. Datta has also observed how *Kari*, in many ways such as these, pushed a lot of boundaries by focusing on the "narrative framework predicated upon interiority" of the female protagonist (2).

Amruta Patil's debut novel *Kari* (2008) was followed by *Adi Parva: Churning of the Ocean* (2012), *Sauptik: Blood and Flowers* (2016) and *Aranyaka: Book of the Forest* (2019), the last novel being a collaboration with Devdutt Pattanaik.

Let us consider the idea of space in the urban settings of *Kari* in contrast to other works of Patil. *Kari* is a story set in an urban city, while other works are primarily Indian mythology-based stories and retellings of Vedic scriptures. The pivotal idea of *Sauptik*, where everyone must quintessentially go into the jungle to get a certain awakening or a perspective, is a reassertion of the metaphorical significance of a forest as a space that imbibes the union of contradiction. It involves perils but also equips those who enter the territory to acquire skills by surviving the odds through the art of allying with hostile forces and acquiring survival codes. The most recent of all, *Aranyaka*, does not emphasise the Vedic stories and the retellings as much as the aura and terrible beauty (to borrow from Yeatsian poetic oxymoronic phrase) of the jungle. Patil chooses to swing the narrative in the ambivalence of the forests' sensuousness as well as the danger it poses for the dweller. *Kari,* however, is set in urban India in the smog city. On the surface, *Kari* departs from other novels in its settings. Is this apparent disjuncture a way to look at *Kari* differently? Kari, the titular queer protagonist, flaneurs through the city spaces and like the pilgrims of the jungle, must battle her fears and awkward moments with the heteronormative conventions of the world. Patil takes upon herself the bold decision to write about the spatiality of even the smog city with love and meticulous focus without judgement.

Most of Patil's themes centre around mythology, but she is extremely conscious of the ecological discourse in the wake of the environmental crisis. She weaves the past stories with the contemporary spatial anxieties posed by hazards of technological and industrial crises embedded in the discourse of pollution and smog. Her novel *Kari* plays naively with the colours of white, black and grey, barring a few coloured pages. This is because as an artist, her shades on the page must be carriers of the darkness of the cityscapes with gutters, sewage, smog and Kari's inevitable role as a boatman. The writer has articulated her affection for sketching Bombay and writing about it with the same profound emotion as her portrayal of Kari, the pioneer of leading heroines in the world of graphic novels.

In the novel's opening pages, where the writer shows Ruth, Kari's beloved, bidding adieu to the city, the readers are shown an aerial view of Bombay. This is Ruth's perspective of the city from the plane, described as "dark and ablaze with fistfuls of light" (Patil 2008, 6). When Ruth flees, Kari is left to live in the city on her own. If the forest in Patil's later works of the duology and *Aranayaka* are the testing grounds of its people, so is the smog city, with an oppressive home, sewage and gutters acting as a laboratory for Kari's life experiment.

Kari is a rich graphic novel that builds upon the problematics of space and place. The binaristic difference between space and place is derived from the feeling that links a person's perception and attitude towards the place rooted in human perception and contact with the spatial zones.

Amruta Patil's *Kari* (2008) is a work of novelty that explores questions of sexuality, layered identities, ambivalent relationships and the alienation of an individual in a vast metro city. All these thematic concerns arise out of the fluid gender discourse where the protagonist, Kari, explores her changing equations with society and its people. In doing so, she is also working out her understanding of the places around her. The writer, who, as a visual artist, made waves in the literary circle, had her own share of struggles back in 2008 when *Kari* dared to make a place for itself in the dominant current of conventions of a reserved society. Kari calls herself "twice-born" (Patil 2008, 41) and this important milestone in the novel resuscitates the promise of life for her after she nearly misses the experience of death because of its confused spatiality. Places such as these simultaneously stand as markers of hope and anxiety. However, topophrenia should not be confused with heterotopia because the latter can refer to any space. Foucault seems to have abandoned it even as his work became more concerned with social spaces in the 1970s. Heterotopia is too broad a term and allows any space as a site of alterity. But topophrenia is invested with human focus as well as interest. The confused spaces come into the present range of writerly works because of the limitations of the binaries of place and non-place. The phrase "talk about Goa" in Bombay is an implicit carrier of the spatial memory of Patil's own experiences of Goa (Patil 2008, 45). Alexa's house, along with the tree and its cat that likes to be seated in a place with an aerial view of the world, opens up topophrenic possibilities. This in-betweenness of place has been discussed by many spatial theorists, including Nicholas Entrikin. Dylan Trigg's disillusionment with the categories of place and non-place arises from his observation that "the bodily experience of place operates on several layers" (Trigg 2017, 130) associating ambiguities with our experience of those places. Such a reading investigates spatiality beyond the extradiegetic spaces (beyond the text) depending upon the perceiver and his world-making endeavours.

Critical concepts such as these then make it possible to celebrate layered spaces because they are emblematic of an unfinished praxis of the mapping project and our ambiguous experience of making sense of the spaces around us. *Kari* expresses the imperative of literary cartography and its fleeting knowledge of the mobile spaces discovered in the acts of flaneuring. "It needs to be mentioned that when I looked for the road to Alexa . . . it was not there . . . but I can never be entirely sure when I will find it next" (Patil 2008, 46). Umberto

Eco (1998), in *Six Walks in the Fictional Woods*, speaks of a similar thing "In order to write this chapter, I walked the same route on several different nights carrying a tape recorder, taking notes on what I could see and what impressions I had" (76). He worked on constructing the real-time and space of a place in Paris. Undoubtedly, there is a fascination for writers to merge the literary space with real geographical locations. However, in a postmodern world, any singular idea of reality is contested that leaves an open fluid ground for multiplicity and metanarratives in literature. Kari's uncertainty about Alexa's house clearly shows that while the house is mapped in mind, its coordinates are not present in the local map of the city. The genius loci of this place are marked by absolute freedom and the quest for knowledge; both unleashed from the act of consciously walking through the cityscapes. Kari feels a "happy buzz" in her pulse that comes out of this flaneuring act (Patil 2008, 46). The mention of Goa implicitly reflects Patil's memory of her homeland, which largely shapes the spirit of space (Goa) merging in the geographical site of Bombay. It comes across as a sweet human endeavour. It gifts her and Laz a fabulous idea for their Fairytale Hair project for the TV commercial.

The problematics of space are found in Kari's outburst, "I cannot reliably tell apart fact from fiction" (Patil 2008, 58) and declarative stance claiming, "my favorite form of movement is float" (70). The narrative of the novel functions as a way to examine how the titular protagonist's flaneuring invites varied ways of seeing the metro city through a gender-fluid lens. Like the *La Passeggiata* tradition of walking in Italy, can Kari's act be linked to the former's teleological role of an attempt for social belonging?

Kari's perception of cityscapes is built with an overarching atmosphere of alienation and feeling lost sentiment. The first time Kari comes to the city, her father advises her, "Don't ever look lost, Ok?" (Patil 2008, 28). This line is instrumental in setting the tone for topophrenic opportunities in the novel. This essential feeling of being out of place is a priori to the topophrenic knowledge of places around us. Though Kari's sense of alienation does not merely come from her position as a migrant, her queerness also comes in the way of socially belonging to the community. She shares the flat with Delna and Billo but has no female bonding. On the other hand, we are told that the urban stench is her companion. She feels it everywhere but cannot fathom its composition. Hence there is a closure needed towards Prakriti, the outside space. Kari's flaneuring contributes to her acceptance of being displaced already and this significantly qualifies her as an ideal urban walker. To understand the urban walk as a wayfinding exercise, let us bring in Benjamin's (1969) discussion on the principal differences between a pedestrian and a flaneur. While investigating both, he built on the resilience and space of the flaneur. Unlike the pedestrian who could be "jostled by the crowd", a flaneur demanded "elbow room" (161).

In the first section, 'The Double Suicide', out of the binarism of light and dark, the dark, stinking sewer saves Kari's life. She admits that in this afterlife, there is no way to come out of it "unscathed" (Patil 2008, 10). The paradox of life after an attempted death is conveyed by Kari in the contradictory presence. She consciously trains herself to breathe scantily as a defence mechanism from the smog that can otherwise damage her lungs. She talks about the necessity to "mutate" (13). Is mutation in any way suggestive of the way to cognitively map her surroundings? Fredrick Jameson's approach to cognitive mapping is a way to cope with the unrepresentable reality by allowing a momentary understanding of places. Within the changing grounds of literary cartographic representations, one must look out for possible alternatives. The beginning point of mutation comes with Kari's sudden desire to map. Robert Tally looks at Heidegger's observations in *Being and Time* (1962) as important pointers to the state of "not-at-homeness" (Tally 2013, 66) which in Spatiality studies, come close to the feeling of human angst, predominantly linked to our sense of place. *Kari* has been discussed with the subject of migration to the city, where it is found that the protagonists in narratives of migration and displacement are found to be lost and disoriented. However, Amruta Patil creatively dwells on the idea of alienation, making that sentiment transition into detachment. The idea of being a boatman is premised on being a bridging link between this world and the otherworldly (afterlife perhaps). Quite crucial to Kari's role as a boatman is the ability to "carry" her own "water" as was suggested by Angel in the Juhu beach horse ride (82). When Angel knows that her death is imminently near, she calls up Kari, saying: "My time is up, boatman. I need you to ferry me over" (102). The symbolism of water carries on throughout the narrative. When Kari finds her "last umbilical cord severed" after seeing Lazarus with his girlfriend Tina, she assumes the clarity from water, asserting that "I know as clear as water what I must do" (110). Kari is aware of the dense ensemble of the place that the smog city is not the floor of the earth that she walks upon. It is a complex assemblage of discourses of culture such as heteronormative conventions of the society, toxic discourse of urbanity, yearnings for female friendships and utopia. Amidst these, Kari feels perplexed with spatial anxieties. While taking up daily commuting, she feels the devouring silence of "railway python" where "no one talks" and stands in the train "two inches from one another and expressionless" (42). Conjoining the menacing aspects of these places is the unsolicited advice that she receives from her flatmates and colleague, Laz. "Eventually a woman needs a man and a man needs a woman" (81) or facing uneasy questions darted at her if she was a "proper lesbian" (79) or utterance from her flatmate, "I want a husband like Kari" (59).

All these instances are suggestive of the challenges and struggles of Kari in Bombay. The term topophrenia is perceived largely with phrenic implications of negative meanings associated with the suffix, but it is important to see the condition of topophrenia not as a disease but as a condition of uneasiness and disease. This then invites places to be lived and navigated through. Kari's boatmanship allows her to comprehend the reality of Crystal Palace with the Snow Globe. One powerful utterance from the novel that can exemplify the simultaneity of place mindedness with the responses of nausea or existential angst is articulated in the dreamy scapes, which Kari finds "fascinating and terrifying at once" (Patil 2008, 48).

Robert Tally in his book on *Spatiality* (2013) sees narratives as mapping machines and ultimately leaves it upon the readers the question of how to situate them based on their own interpretative subjectivities. In the project of spatially mapping the novel *Kari*, one looks at the places in the text as gateways to arrive at topophrenic possibilities. Tally, in the titular book on Topophrenia, defines the titular term as a necessary condition to bring out effective geographies. It does not mean that this will lead us to arrive at the truth of the places. But with the awareness of the place that topophrenia generates, comprehending spatial experience becomes possible. More significantly, any affective geography, according to Tally, must not shy away from communicating uneasiness, fear, nausea or angst because it is so much a part of understanding spatial contours around us.

Kari incorporates in herself the oxymoronic awareness of the risk involved in living with her sexuality in the big city's clogged habitat. She articulates herself as a specimen of paradoxical geography, where the simultaneity of centre and margin, inner fox and fish, subjectivity with objective knowledge of the dense patterns of places exists. She says, "I am a treacherous dangerous fish. I have smooth fins and very sharp teeth" (Patil 2008, 85).

Topophrenia shows limitless potential to transform the places where we live through the story embedded in the narratives. It is also a way to imagine the world differently. If topophrenia is the inclusive condition of knowing the menacing aspects of a place, it does not give up on the mapping praxis. In *Kari,* the painful and unpleasant responses to places and spaces are invoked by the relations of space and individuals. Ruth's separation and death of Angel shatter her and snake-like figures in the text are signs of cautioning her to hold back. She steps out, nonetheless. Like any other species, Kari is comfortable in inhabiting her body, knowing no shame. She fights for her fluidity against the flaming walls of sexuality and fixidity. The brilliance of Kari as a path-breaking heroine in the comic world is striking with its quietness. The desire to break free is reflected in the way the pages of the book are loosely patterned. To convey a fluid story like this, which went into the public domain without clear labels, the writer succeeded in feeding the cultural and literary space of the times with its quietness and lack of propaganda.

One of the greatest hallmarks of this novel is that through topophrenic lens and cognitive mapping, there is a celebration of the seeker, who, in her queerness, does not feel the need to decimate her body for a higher quest. The physical environment is as real as her quest and hunger. So is the real-imagined Snow Globe and spatiality of Grotty kitchen and evolving spaces like the Secret Garden. If we think of topophrenia as a kind of place mindedness, then we could imagine a place seeming to be a place of otherness to some and not to others. For example, a zoo contains exotic animals while being at the heart of a quotidian domestic space. Liminality (of home as oppressive with the simultaneity of kitchen garden) and otherworldliness (of alterity) should strike the readers as also having marvellous connections and distinctions, as having the threshold experience. It is, by definition, also a moment of transgression or crossing over that implies alterity again. Topophrenia takes us from a strange movement, from familiar to unfamiliar. In *Kari*, through these oscillations, the readers become aware of newer spatialities that can be mapped, even though they may not have clear signposts or map pointers. In doing so, one inevitably creates the possibilities of alternate worlds.

Works Cited

Benjamin, Walter. 1969. "On Some Motifs in Baudelaire." In *Illuminations: Essays and Reflections*. Edited by Hannah Arendt. Translated by Harry Zohn, 155–200. New York: Schocken Books.

Datta, Surangama. 2020. "'Can You See Her the Way I Do?': (Feminist) Ways of Seeing in Amruta Patil's *Kari* (2008)." *Feminist Encounters: A Journal of Critical Studies in Culture and Politics* 4 (1). https://doi.org/10.20897/femenc/7917.

Eco, Umberto. 1998. *Six Walks in the Fictional Woods*. Harvard University Press.

Foucault, Michel, and Jay Miskowiec. 1986. "Of Other Spaces." *Diacritics* 16 (1): 22–27. https://doi.org/10.2307/464648.

Freud, Sigmund. 2010. *Civilisation and its Discontents*. Translated by James Strachey. New York: W.W. Norton.

Harvey, David. 1990. *The Condition of Postmodernity*. Oxford: Blackwell.

Heidegger, Martin. 1962. *Being and Time*. Translated by John Macquarrie and Edward Robinson. New York: Harper and Row.

Jameson, Fredric. 1991. *Postmodernism, or, the Cultural Logic of Late Capitalism*, Durham, NC: Duke University Press.

Junoon - A Stage for Theatre. 2019. "Mumbai Local with Amruta Patil." https://www.youtube.com/watch?v=1srFJCRpaoY.

Lefebvre, Henri. 1991. *The Production of Space*. Translated by Donald Nicholson-Smith. Oxford: Blackwell.

Lukacs, Georg. 1971. *The Theory of the Novel*. Translated by Anna Bostock. Cambridge, M.A: The MIT Press.

Lyotard, Jean-François. 1984. "The Postmodern Condition: A Report on Knowledge." Translated by Geoff Bennington and Brian Massumi. *Poetics Today* 5 (4): 886. https://doi.org/10.2307/1772278.

Massey, Doreen. 2005. *For Space*. London: Sage.

Patil, Amruta. 2008. *Kari*. New Delhi: Harper Collins Publishers India.

Said, Edward. 1978. *Orientalism*, New York: Vintage.

Sartre, Jean-Paul. 1964. *Nausea*. Translated by Lloyd Alexander. New York: New Directions.

Schwarz, Gretchen. 2002. "Graphic Novels for Multiple Literacies." *Journal of Adolescent & Adult Literacy* 46 (3): 262–65. https://eric.ed.gov/?id=EJ655342.

Soja, Edward W. 1996. *Thirdspace: Journeys to Los Angeles and other Real-and-Imagined Places*, Oxford: Blackwell.

Tally, Robert T. 1996. "Jameson's Project of Cognitive Mapping: A Critical Engagement." Edited by Rolland G. Paulston.

Social Cartography: Mapping Ways of Seeing Social and Educational Change, 399–416. New York: Garland.

———. 2014. *Literary Cartographies. Palgrave Macmillan US EBooks*. https://doi.org/10.1057/9781137449375.

———. 2019. *Topophrenia: Place, Narrative, and the Spatial Imagination*. Indiana University Press, 2019.

Trigg, Dylan. 2017. "Place and Non-Place: A Phenomenological Perspective." In *Contributions to Hermeneutics*, 127–39. Springer International Publishing. https://doi.org/10.1007/978-3-319-52214-2_10.

Tuan, Yi-Fu. 1977. *Space and Place: The Perspective of Experience*. Minneapolis: University of Minnesota Press.

Westphal, Bertrand. 2011. *Geocriticism: Real and Fictional Spaces*. Translated by Robert T. Tally Jr. New York: Palgrave Macmillan.

William, Raymond. 1973. *The Country and the City*, Oxford: Oxford University Press.

Woolf, Virginia. 1986. "Literary Geography." In *The Essays of Virginia Woolf*. Edited by Andrew McNeillie. 158–61. Orlando: Harcourt.

5

Psychological Trauma Through Efficacious Visualisation: A Study of *Hush*

S. Sri Sakuntala

Introduction

Graphic novels have become an acceptable part of literature as an outstanding medium of expression. Graphic novels are a single narrative told through "drawings, illustrations, and sometimes photos" (Scholastic Parents Staff 2023). The graphic representations are not only confined then to daily newspapers in the form of comic gear and cartoon sketches but have also metamorphosed into more mature forms. According to a Britannica report, "For many, the word *comics* denotes a periodical for children" so, these writings are regarded as cheap, undermined, entertainment for children or sub-literature. In the past few years, this medium of expression has changed gradually (Murray 2017). This genre encompasses far more than the comic books with which it is most commonly associated. Graphic novels are becoming increasingly popular among readers of all ages. Graphic novels are not only a vehicle for all subaltern revolt voices but also act as a voice of rebellion that blurs the lines between the subaltern and the mainstream. It includes all of India's everyday rebellious stories and protesting voices. This decade's graphic novels investigate various ways of representing one's identity and culture in a matrix of silenced voices. Through the revisioning of mythologies, post-millennial graphic novels express a plethora of suppressed voices.

Numerous effective reading skills are needed to read a graphic novel, let alone a wordless one, including the ability to understand a sequence of events, interpret characters' nonverbal gestures, discern the story's outcome and make inferences. Students can learn correlation and comprehension skills through graphic novels, which they can apply when interacting with pictures, portraits and people.

The Graphic Novel Phenomenon Has Reached India

Looking at the genre's history and evolution can help us better understand it. The modern Indian graphic novel fundamentally repositions and brings the comics medium into the twenty-first century. They have been published by smaller picture book publishers like political press Navayana and the Tara Books, comics-only publishers like Manta Ray, Phantomville and Blaft, and significant general publishing houses like Harper Collins, Hachette and Penguin.

The phrase graphic novel was coined in English in 1964 and popularised by American legend Will Eisner. It can be simply defined as a "big comic" in book form aimed at modern readers, and graphic novels are considered "an emerging new literature of our times" (Campbell 2007, 13). A graphic novel, according to Art Spiegelman, is a "comic that is substantial enough to require a bookmark" (Gravett 2015) such as his Pulitzer Prize-winning *Maus* (1986). In this regard, India has joined the movement. A growing collection of non-genre Indian graphic novels arose as a thriving phenomenon at the start of the twenty-first century.

The first Indian comic book series, *Amar Chitra Katha*, is where the history of Indian graphic novels began. It is a comic book series created by Anant Pai in 1967. Gulshan Rai founded Diamond Comics, an ancillary publishing firm in 1978. The publishing house arose from its parent company, Bharatiya Bhandar Pustakalaya, which was founded in Pakistan following the partition in 1907. *Chacha Chaudhary*, *Billoo*, *Pinki*, and *Motu Patlu* were among their early publications. They later began publishing foreign comic book series in Hindi, including *Phantom*, *Mandrake*, *Superman*, *Batman*, *Spider-Man*, *He-Man*, and *James Bond*. Raj Comics is India's other famous comic publishing firm. They are essential in the development of the desi superhero and the production of Hindi comic books.

River of Stories by Orijit Sen was published in 1994, just before the end of the century as a successor to comic strips. It showed the social and political issues that arose during the construction of a dam along the Narmada River. Because of the impact of Western graphic novels as a result of globalisation and rising consumer culture, India now has its own publishing houses. Pop Culture Publishing House, Vimanika Comics, Campfire Comics, Arkin Comics, Liquid Comics, and Level 10 are among the leading graphic novel publishers as a result. Leading publishing giants such as Penguin and Harper Collins later entered the sector with their groundbreaking, trend-setting graphic books. As in the self-published anthology Comix, graphic novels published in the 2000s depicted everyday life stories of love, hate, lust, and creed. *Anthologies from India* (2008-2009) and *Kabul Disco* (2009) also represented the politicised aspect of an individual narrative, as in Amruta Patil's *Kari* (2008) and Parismita Singh's *Hotel at the End of the World* (2009). They also expressed alternative viewpoints by revising Indian mythology, legends, and folklore, as in *Devi* (2007, 2008) by Shekar Kapur and Virgin Comics.

Reading a Graphic Novel

The graphic novel is significantly new to literature. As a part of fictional and non-fictional writings, the visual narrative of a story brings high effectiveness. The graphic novel contains only a few words with diagrammatic presentations. Readers, particularly children, show more interest in reading these stories. When students read a graphic novel, their brains are more active in analysing the concept "with an analytical eye, depth and complexity are added to the reading process" (Morrison 2017). When students read the visual narration, their brain gets more active than reading the theoretical text.

Students see the images and figures, connect them, and build a story, "this includes the plot, narrative, character development, problem, and resolution" (Baigelman 2022). One can interpret pictures in different ways, improving their utmost capabilities in thinking. In a traditional way of learning, students generally try to know the meaning of a word written already while reading a story. But while reading a graphic story, students think about the context of the text and relate words according to the situation. This means they try to think about the meaning and later search for suitable words that fit into the context. Graphic novels help students connect with various objects and try to connect the situations according to the context.

The Implication of Sketches and Figures in *Hush*

Hush (2011) by Pratheek Thomas, illustrated by Rajiv Eipe, is a wordless graphic novel. "Some things are not meant to be spoken about" is the tagline of *Hush*. This line creates apprehension about the story. The images in the text create terror and grab the readers' attention. Symbolism is the main feature of this graphic novel (Mehale 2011). The grey, black and white sketches tell a unique kind of story. This kind of artistic visualisation brings panic and harsh effects to the story (Aravind 2012). From the images in the text, we infer that this is the story of a young girl named Maya. We can observe that she has been a victim of child sexual abuse at the hands of her father. The theme is about how a child breaks her silence after suffering sexual violence.

One day, Maya enters the vice principal's office in the school. She sees a girl sitting in the corner of a table in the office, just opposite the principal. The girl is very terrified and shrinks with folded hands as she speaks through her eyes to tell us that the principal is ill-treating her. He threatens the girl to not open her mouth with intimidating actions.

Later, she recalls the incidents that happened at her home. The mental trauma drives her almost mad. She became increasingly lonely due to past incidents. It is seen that Maya is "holding a gun with a smoking barrel, poised, teary-eyed and silent like the rest of her classmates whose astonishment, horror and fear are written on their faces" (Singh 2011). The girl brought a gun to the school and killed someone, which astonished all the students in the class. We can see the horror on the faces of the students who are sitting behind her in the class. We can observe the bullet pierced the head of a dead person, whose blood drenched the blackboard and formed a spider web of broken shards.

We can find that there is no happiness on Maya's face. Her mother knew about her husband's cruel nature, but she could not stop him from entering Maya's bedroom to molest her as she feared his aggressive behaviour and had remained silent all her life. Maya and her mother are both victims of a man's aggression. Even if children do not speak about abuse, they might indicate that something major and distressing has occurred to them in nonverbal ways. A problem could be characterised by significant or abrupt changes in mood or behaviour. Sadness, tearfulness, lethargy, irritability or mood fluctuations are all possible indicators of depression. Children may also begin to isolate themselves, retreating from family and friends and spending all of their time away from home. This sexual abuse left Maya in depression and her thoughts moved into a hushed tone. She stands alone in the pictures, indicating that her thoughts were filled with fear, agony and insecurity.

Her mental illness leads to the murder of the accused person with a gun, whose body lies behind the classroom table. She finally kills herself before the police apprehends her, so the intensity of her depression stands in silence forever.

Psychological Impact on the Survivors

Sexual violence has far-reaching consequences that go beyond physical injuries, regardless of age or gender. The trauma of being sexually assaulted or raped can be life-changing, leaving one feeling terrified, ashamed, alone and plagued by nightmares, flashbacks and other unpleasant memories. The world no longer appears to be a secure environment for the victims as they no longer have faith in others. They may begin to doubt others' judgement, self-worth and sometimes even their sanity. Relationships feel perilous and intimacy is out of the question.

Furthermore, like many rape survivors, they may suffer from anxiety, depression and "frequently experience symptoms of post-traumatic stress disorder (PTSD)" (World Health Organisation, 2003, 15). It is important to remember that they are going through a normal reaction to trauma. They suffer from the symptoms: feelings of helplessness, shame, inadequacy and self-blame.

Sexual abuse is a severe health hazard that causes different disorders to victims, especially children. Depression is the main problem that haunts them throughout their life. Sometimes these mental issues affect physical activities, leading to a low rate of physical growth in children. Similarly, "emotional and psychological symptoms have long-lasting effects" (Radmanovic 2020, S350). The victims develop a negative attitude in their lives because of unbearable events. They do not like to participate in any activities, which is a significant obstacle to social participation. Post-traumatic stress disorder is another consequence of sexual abuse in children and children who have experienced sexual abuse show behavioural and emotional changes. Consequently, the high factors in sexual violence include "symptoms of depression, anxiety and post-traumatic stress disorder" (Rohan 2018). However, anger, fear and anxiety are all examples of possible emotions. Some people may experience shock and numbness, while others may mask their feelings and act as if everything is fine. We can observe in the pictures that the face of Maya is portrayed with a broad open-eyed and serious look. This symbolises her agony and antipathy.

One of the most challenging things to deal with following an assault by someone you know is the violation of trust. Moreover, it is horrible that a person is victimised by immediate family members like the father, brother or uncle. Maya has post-traumatic stress disorder due to this incident. She cannot move forward because her father makes her feel very insecure at home. This act of harassment leads to Maya's attempted suicide, which seems to be the only way to quell the burning issue that lies inside her.

Conclusion

Many people feel utterly powerless after being raped or sexually assaulted. Sexual assault victims may find it difficult to talk about what happened, while others may need to discuss the incident again. One might help them regain control and encourage them to seek assistance. Victims need advice from their loved ones on proceeding and getting back from the horrendous situation. *Hush* reveals and narrates factual incidents through pictures because only action can demonstrate more than a thousand words. The way of representing the story through efficacious drawing helps the study and envision a story with the utmost attention. The study of *Hush* reveals Maya's silence, agony, violence and frustration. These are actual events that happen in society. Representing real incidents as a story in graphic novels educates people, especially children. Sexual violence has a wide range of health consequences, including both psychological and physical effects in the short and long term. Perhaps most importantly, sexual abuse can have devastating long-term psychological effects, influencing and drastically altering a person's entire life course.

Works Cited

Amar Chitra Katha. 2023. "'So What Is Amar Chitra Katha?'" Amar Chitra Katha. https://www.amarchitrakatha.com/about-us/.

Aravind, Aju. 2012. "Review of Hush by Pratheek Thomas." *Lapis Lazuli–An International Literary Journal* II (I). http://pintersociety.com/wp-content/uploads/2012/04/Reviewed-by-Dr.-Aju-Aravind.pdf.

Baigelman, Louise. 2022. "Why Graphic Novels Are Good for Struggling Readers." *Understood*, March. https://www.understood.org/articles/en/5-reasons-graphic-novels-can-help-kids-with-reading.

Campbell, Eddie. 2007. "What Is a Graphic Novel?" *World Literature Today* 81 (2).

Gravett, Paul. 2015. "The Indian Graphic Novel Is Here to Stay." British Council. October 29, 2015. https://www.britishcouncil.org/voices-magazine/indian-graphic-novel-here-stay.

Hammond, Heidi. 2009. *Graphic Novels and Multimodal Literacy: A Reader Response Study*. University of Minnesota. https://conservancy.umn.edu/bitstream/11299/48560/1/Hammond_umn_0130E_10225.pdf.

Mahale, Sneha. 2011. "Time to Get Graphic about Social Issues." *Hindustan Times*. https://www.hindustantimes.com/books/time-to-get-graphic-about-social-issues/story-ik1vJURX2ggcp7jR5FSwFL.html.

Morrison, Leslie. 2017. "The Research Behind Graphic Novels and Young Learners." *Northwestern Center for Talent Development* (blog). https://www.ctd.northwestern.edu/blog/research-behind-graphic-novels-and-young-learners.

Murray, Christopher. 2023. "Graphic Novel | History, Genres & Impact." Encyclopedia Britannica. April 10, 2023. https://www.britannica.com/art/graphic-novel.

Radmanovi , Marija Burgi . 2020. "Mental Disorders in Sexually Abused Children." *Psychiatria Danubina* 32 (October): 349–52. https://pubmed.ncbi.nlm.nih.gov/33030451/.

Rohan, Alicia. 2018. "Study Explains Why Some Childhood Abuse Victims Develop Certain Mental Illnesses - News." *UAB News*, October. https://www.uab.edu/news/research/item/9826-study-explains-why-some-childhood-abuse-victims-develop-certain-mental-illnesses.

Singh, Jairaj. 2011. "Muted and Macabre." *Hindustan Times*, January 7, 2011. https://www.hindustantimes.com/books/muted-and-macabre/story-U5nh7ZabkzymWTnc9jZ9DJ.html.

Spiegelman, Art. 1986, *Maus*. New York: Pantheon Books.

Scholastic Parents Staff. 2023. "3 Ways Graphic Novels Benefit Reading Skills." *Scholastic*, March. https://www.scholastic.com/parents/books-and-reading/raise-a-reader-blog/3-reasons-graphic-novels-can-be-great-young-readers.html.

"The National Child Traumatic Stress Network." n.d. The National Child Traumatic Stress Network. https://nctsn.org/.

Thomas, Pratheek. 2010. *Hush: Some Things Are Not Meant to Be Talked About*. Bangalore: Manta Ray.

World Health Organisation. 2003. *Guidelines for Medico-Legal Care for Victims of Sexual Violence*. https://apps.who.int/iris/handle/10665/42788.

6

Amruta Patil's *Kari*: Marginalised Non-Heterosexual in Normalised Heterosexual Metropolitan City

M. Sri Varshni and V. Sunitha

According to Merriam-Webster's Dictionary, the term graphic novel is defined as "a fictional story that is presented in comic-strip format and published as a book". The term graphic novel was first coined in 1964 by a historian named Richard Kyle in one of his essays. Later, the term gained popularity with the publication of Will Eisner's *A Contract with God* (1982) and Marvel's *Graphical Line* (1982), which brought the comics to the public's attention. It was in 2001 that the book industry began to use graphic novels as a category in bookstores.

Graphic novels have risen to prominence as a result of comic books. However, they differ in tone, as Lila Christensen (2006) pointed out that "in contrast to superhero comic books, graphic novels are more serious, often nonfiction, full-length, sequential art novels that explore the issues of race, social justice, global conflict, and war with intelligence and humor" (227). Graphic novels, as sequential art, convey a story with multiple images in conjunction with text arranged in sequence to form a story. Since it brings the discriminated voices of society along with the visual representation in this digital world, the graphic novels of this period discuss numerous issues related to gender, sexuality, identity, race and marginality.

According to Gravett (2015), Indian comics were "under-appreciated as cheap, undemanding, throwaway entertainment mainly for kids or the sub-literate". Since 1967, comics in India have become a serious business. The publication of the *Amar Chitra Katha* series and *Tinkle* comics somewhat changed the perception of comics by adapting legends and histories from Indian epics and mythologies to demonstrate the importance of comics for children.

The River of Stories (1994), written by Orijit Sen, a pioneer of the genre, comment on a recurring theme of the socio-political issue, which is Adivasis displacement due to the construction of Sardar Sarovar Dam. Sarnath Banerjee, the most prominent graphic novelist of India, visualises the common setting of urban India with the idea of fractured realities and the invisible lives of a Delhi shopkeeper in his first graphic book, *Corridor* (2004). The situation of Dalits is contextualised by revisiting Dr. B. R. Ambedkar's life in *Bhimayana: Experience of Untouchability* (2011), a book written by Srividya Natarajan and S. Anand and illustrated by Gond artist Durgabai and Subhash Vyam. Ambedkar was a great legislator and an untouchable himself. In his book *The Delhi Calm*, published in 2010, writer Vishwajyoti Ghosh decodes the president's declaration of a state of emergency from 1975 to 1977. Amruta Patil's *Kari*, published in 2008, gained the name as the first Indian lesbian graphic novel that speaks on sexual minorities in society. Srividhya Natrajan, S. Anand, Abdul Sultan, Subhadra Sen Gupta, Vishwajyoti Ghosh, Parismita Singh, Vidyun Sabhaney, Tapash Guha and Naseer Ahmed are the people who have kept the Indian heritage and tradition alive in the form of modern graphic narratives.

By exploring mythologies, old histories and religious texts, graphic novels can portray the status of depressed voices of sex, gender, race and class. Through its rich ancient heritage of visual narratives, Indian graphic novels have contributed colour to the transcultural graphic phenomena and they think that successful communication would be achieved through visual imagery. As a result of British colonialism, new forms of visual tales became popular in the early twentieth century. The elements were combined and India developed its particular style, emphasising its historical and cultural nuances. According to Prorokova (2018), ". . . Keeping in line with some of the Western characteristics of the comics, graphic narratives in Asia have dealt with domestic, historical and contemporary events, including western colonialism, and their own religious ideas, local politics, and domestic social process" (4).

Amruta Patil is a writer and painter by profession, born on 19 April 1979 in Pune. Her notable works include *Kari* (2008), *Adi Parva: Churning of the Ocean* (2012), *Sauptik: Blood and Flower* (2016) and *Aranyaka: Book of the Forest* (2019). She has a freewheeling visual style in her novels that includes many recurring themes like sexuality, myth, identity and sustainable living. She was influenced by visual art from her childhood stories of *Amar Chitra Katha*, temple art, Mughal miniature and Indian mythology. As a pioneer in Indian graphic novels, Patil serves as an archetype to many writers of the generation. She was awarded the Nari Shakti Puraskar in March 2017 for her "unusual work that breaks boundaries". Marielle Morin, a book attaché at the French embassy in Delhi, says, "Amruta is a unique and distinctive voice, both aesthetically and stylistically. She's a gifted writer and an astonishing visual artist, and that combination is rare. She can't be put under any label" (Menezes 2021).

Kari by Amruta Patil is a landmark work that deals with the problems associated with the societal concept of gender. Kari's life as a non-heterosexual identity in a normalised heteronormative metropolitan city is examined. The writer shows her exceptional balance between the lines (words) and the visuals (images). *Kari* has earned the merit of the first graphic Indian novel by an Indian woman. It is also considered a text that elaborates on the themes of sexuality, gender and homophobic culture. Surangama Datta (2008) observes and comments on *Kari* as a culturally important text:

The remarkable quality of this work lies not only in its status as first, but in the way its experimental form and content introduce new ways of perceiving and visualising experience, in this case, that of a queer woman, bringing innovative possibilities into the Indian graphic arena. For instance, its keen understanding of female spaces and homosocial interactions (such as Kari's relations with various women in the text, the interpersonal dynamic between her female flatmates, Billo and Delna), questions of gender performance and non-conformity, Kari's complex friendship with dying cancer patient Angel, her love for Ruth, allows for an interesting study of gender in the contemporary context (1).

Sexual and gender minorities are compelled to fit into a cultural construct of gender and sexuality. Kari's identification as a non-heterosexual in a normalised heterosexual population, as well as the themes of friendship, heartbreak and dismissing a non-binary as unfit for society to exist, are all explored in *Kari.*

Kari is a significant work in Indian graphical history. At 29, while working in an ad agency, Patil created her eponymous heroin Kari, an alter ego subconsciously developed from her own experience. This work also makes her debut as a coming of age because Patil saw the light of day a decade ago. At the time, there wasn't a ubiquitous gender dialogue as today. Patil herself declared about Kari, "I think it was a coming-of-age thing for Indian young adult literature". "Urban investigation of sexuality and psychology" is how Kari describes herself (Patil 2012). "Kari is a young, deeply introverted, asocial and queer woman, a counterpoint to the hyper-feminine prototypes you keep coming across".

Feminism is a political movement that started as an ideology insisting on the social, political, and economic rights of women in society. Feminism as a movement talks about gender and its role for the first time in English literature and it is reflected in the works of most writers of the past and present. As quoted by P.T. Barnum in his *The Humbugs of the World* (1866), "Literature is one of the most interesting and significant expressions of humanity" (13). The development of feminist theory also introduced an umbrella term called LGBT (Lesbian Gay Bisexual Transgender) society and marked the beginning of queer studies. Queer studies, as a field of literature, began in the 1990s and is still expanding with new ideologies and theories. The earliest recorded meaning of the word queer, according to the Oxford English Dictionary, is 'strange, odd, peculiar, eccentric'. There are only a few words in the English lexicon which picked up a negative meaning for centuries. By 1567, the word queer meant bad, despicable, worthless and untrustworthy. In 1781, it mutated into a verb, 'to spoil or ruin'. It is rarely acknowledged that the first recorded usage of the word queer referring to men who love men were found in an infamous letter by John Douglas, the ninth Marquess of Queensberry, in 1894. By 1914, queer, as a descriptive term for sexually non-conforming individuals, gained popularity and began to appear in print media. In 1914, the Oxford English Dictionary cited an article from the Los Angeles Times that described a club as "composed of the 'queer' people," where "the 'queer' people have a good time" (Maccabe and Yanacek 2018). The term queer is gaining positive political currency, even though there is opposition to it. The lesbian and gay literary theory emerged prominently as a distinct field only by the 1990s. The emergence and acceptance of an individual field named lesbian and gay studies prove the growing significance of women's studies.

The term homosexual is itself a medical term, first used in 1869 Germany and preceding the invention of the corresponding term heterosexual by eleven years. The issues of gender identity are different from the issues of sexual orientation. Gender identity includes gender binary, gender identity, gender pronoun, genderqueer/non-binary gender, gender questioning, intersex, sister girl/brother boy and transgender/gender diversity. On the other hand, sexual orientation includes lesbian, gay, bisexual, asexual and pansexual.

LGBTIQA+ is an acronym for lesbian, gay, bisexual, transgender, intersexual, queer, asexual and ally. Gender identity is a person's personal perception of their sex, which might be their sex at birth or diverge from it. Gender expression and gender identity carry two separate meanings. In gender expression, there is only an external expression in the way of attitude, behaviour and dressing based on the scale of masculinity and femininity. Lesbian, gay, bisexual and asexual people come under sexual orientations; that is, a person's sexual identity is related to the gender to which they are attracted. Homosexuals, heterosexuals and bisexuals are to be brought into this sexual orientation. Intersex and transgender are based on their gender identity. Intersex may also be of biological sex in some rare cases. For example, a person may look like a female from the outside but have the anatomy of a male from the inside.

Judith Butler, a notable gender theorist, distinguishes between biological sex and cultural gender in her work *Bodies that Matters: On the Discursive Limitation of "Sex,"* published in 2011. However, when viewed through the lens of gender, the body (sex) is problematic. According to Butler, sex is a perfect construct rather than a fixed object. Butler interprets that regulatory or cultural norms lead to the appearance of bodies over time. Regulatory power is not an external imposition of power on a subject but it is an operative constraint in the subject's very formation (Butler 2011, 33).

Kari's central protagonist is gender and sexually-diverse. The novel opens with a double suicidal attempt by Kari and her partner Ruth; the force behind their decision was their queerness. After they are rescued by the net and sewer, the story follows the flashback and afterlife of Kari in the "smog city" (Patil 2008, 13). She was exposed to the dark heart of the smog city. *Kari* is much more than a non-binary novel; it is a view of the society we inhabit. It reflects the social condition that presumes gender roles and tries to fit into them. "It is a deeply moving narrative centred around the search for self in this increasingly dominating society mired in difference and discrimination" (Mahurkar 2017). The book tries to depict the lived realities of homosexuals in a normalised heterosexual society. The graphic illustration of a queer figure can be situated anywhere in the world. However, it references a specific geographical area in which the subject of sexual orientation explains the author's social realities. According to Cohen, "Both localised practises and centralised institutions legitimise and privilege heterosexuality and heterosexual relationships as fundamental and natural within society" (448).

The naturalised and oppressing nature of hetero culture is evident in many parts of this novel. To be noted are some of Kari's conversations with the two men—Orgo and Zap, boyfriends of her roommates. They urge Kari to find a perfect man for herself. Moreover, the boys also insist that "Eventually a woman needs a man and a man needs a woman" (Patil 2008, 81). Orgo goes further to search for a match for her, "Laz is such a great guy. You have so much in common, both of you are into books and don't party" (81). This demonstrates how the cultural guardians have manipulated and normalised the term heterosexual as natural and common to all. In another instance, Lazarus, a coworker and a trainee art director in her ad agency, asks Kari, "Are you, like, a proper Lesbian?" (79). Kari thinks about the question, "I roll the word 'lesbian' in my mouth and it feels strange there. Sort of fleshly, salivating, fresh off the boat from Lesbia, and totally inappropriate" (79). This inquiry about her sexuality appears to be a safe one to ask because it reflects the normalisation of heterosexuality, in which non-heterosexual actions and desires are virtually eradicated and stigmatised.

In another instance, Kari's parents come to her apartment to meet her. They have internalised the concept of normal sexuality. When someone remains outside the box of the dominant social norms, rules and regulations, they are considered unintelligible. Her parents want her to be in the intelligible patterns of society. It is suggested that Kari tries to tell her parents about her sexual orientation. Her mom replied, "This is not how I raised you . . . of all the people in such a big city you pick the smut and the degenerates" (31). Queer is a pejorative or term before them because of its negative historical derogatory connotations. Kari is depressed and says, "what you call smut is someone else's ache and reality, mamma" and ends by saying that "this city has made a boatman of me" (31). Her family fears that she may get ostracised and compel her to repress her lesbian identity, asking her to act as a 'straight' person in front of society.

The alienation of the homosexual in a heterosexual society can be exposed clearly through the presence of the sewer in the novel. The sewer is sketched in a grey hue on the pages that depict its marginality and the indifference of people towards it. Likewise, the people in the metropolitan city are not aware of the sewer, as homophobic society is also unaware of the crisis, pain and dilemma of homosexuals. These incidents that happen in Kari's life display the constructed notion of sex, gender and sexuality by the heteronormative society. Butler (1999) contends that desire and sexuality are unrelated to sex or gender and works to dismantle conventional ideas of sexuality and gender in order to create new avenues for subject matter that does not fit inside the heterosexual framework. The isolation and emptiness in her life continue to travel in her second birth "I, Kari, twice-born, who trawl the drains dream after dream, can smell the sewer everywhere" (Patil 2008, 41). But the isolation was doubled after the separation from Ruth. "I give my days to the ad agency, work like a fury and sleep like the dead" (14).

Angel and Lazarus bring Kari back to her present after her heartbreak with Ruth. Angel, a dying cancer patient, appears to be a girl who gives importance to her gender attitude. During a conversation with Kari, Angel reveals herself. "I am bald because I'm sick not because I'm butch" (Patil 3008, 38). Angel's long hair represents her gender role and her position in society. Hair is important in the novel in defining gender roles, particularly in the Indian context. Long hair is inextricably linked to patriarchal definitions of female entities. Hair is important in the novel in defining gender roles, particularly in the Indian context. Long hair is inextricably linked to patriarchal definitions of female entities. Angel, who is feminine in gender, considers her lack of long hair to be a great loss. The strong relationship between Lazarus and Angel reveals Kari's gender expression as non-binary. Kari's act of expressing her gender creates confusion about her identity. Finally, she is identified as non-binary in the last chapter. Her consistent hard work brings her the creative award. In the public gathering, she decided to show her identity with a 2mm buzz cut. To quote Butler, "For a gay or lesbian identity-position to sustain its appearance as coherent, heterosexuality must remain in that rejected and repudiated place" (Butler 1993, 113).

The novel all the way goes with suicide for the second time. The Pigeon Girl from the fifth floor climbs the water tank across and jumps to her death in the last pages, just as Kari considers jumping from the building as well. This phase of recalling her act in the story begins "when one's performative gender performs various acts; it makes the incoherent "discourses" understandable through the acts it does" (Raju 2021, 93). Kari makes her strong confirmation this time "1) I feel no bird urge. 2) I want to step back, not step off. 3) I still love Ruthie more than anyone else in the world, but I won't be jumping off ledges for anyone for anymore" (Patil 2008, 115).

Through the novel, Kari's search for her identity as a woman in the normalised, heteronormative metropolitan society tells the position of social and unconscious biases that they might harbour too. The study brought out the normative and constructed role of gender and sexuality through the character Kari, even before non-binary became a standard term in the pre-pride period. Kari's constant action of defining her identity shows the darker side of our cities as an alien land for gender and sexual minorities.

Works Cited

Barnum, Phineas Taylor. 1866. *The Humbugs of the World*. New York: Carleton Publishers.

Butler, Judith. 1993. *Bodies That Matter: On the Discursive Limits of "Sex."* London and New York: Routledge. https://www2.warwick.ac.uk/fac/arts/english/currentstudents/pg/masters/modules/femlit/bodies-that-matter.pdf.

———. 1999. *Gender Trouble: Feminism and the Subversion of Identity*. Routledge.

Christensen, Lila L. 2006. "Graphic Global Conflict: Graphic Novels in the High School Social Studies Classroom." *The Social Studies* 97 (6): 227–30. https://doi.org/10.3200/tsss.97.6.227-230.

Cohen, Cathy. 1997. "Punks, Bulldaggers, and Welfare Queens: The Radical Potential of Queer Politics?" *GLQ: A Journal of Lesbian and Gay Studies* 3 (4): 437–65. https://doi.org/10.1215/10642684-3-4-437.

Datta, Surangama. 2020. "'Can You See Her the Way I Do?': (Feminist) Ways of Seeing in Amruta Patil's *Kari* (2008)." *Feminist Encounters: A Journal of Critical Studies in Culture and Politics* 4 (1). https://doi.org/10.20897/femenc/7917.

"Definition of Graphic Novel." 2023. In *Merriam-Webster Dictionary*. https://www.merriam-webster.com/dictionary/graphic%20novel.

Ghosh, Vishwajyoti. 2010. *Delhi Calm*. New Delhi: Harper Collins.

Gravett, Paul. 2012. "Amruta Patil: India's First Female Graphic Novelist." September 2012. http://www.paulgravett.com/articles/article/amruta_patil.

———. 2015. "The Indian Graphic Novel Is Here to Stay." British Council. October 29, 2015. https://www.britishcouncil.org/voices-magazine/indian-graphic-novel-here-stay.

Maccabe, Colin, and Holly Yanacek. 2018. "From 'Odd,' "strange," and 'Bad,' to Reclaiming the Word 'Queer.'" *Oxford University Press*, December. https://blog.oup.com/2018/12/lgbtq-community-reclaiming-the-word-queer/.

Mahurkar, Vaishnavi. 2017. "Kari: A Graphic Novel About Lesbianism and Big-City Love." *Feminism in India*, April. https://feminisminindia.com/2017/03/28/kari-book-review/.

Menezes, Vivek. 2021. "India's First Female Graphic Novelist Amruta Patil Is Graphing the Future." *GQ India*, July 26, 2021. https://www.gqindia.com/get-smart/content/india-first-female-graphic-novelist-amruta-patil-graphing-the-future.

Patil, Amruta. 2008. *Kari*. Harper Collins.

———. 2012. *Adi Parva*. Harper Collins.

———. 2016. *Sauptik: Blood and Flowers*. Harper Collins.

Patil, Amruta, and Devdutt Pattanaik. 2019. *Aranyaka: Book of the Forest*. Westland. .

Vyam, Durgabai, Srividya Natarajan, Subhash Vyam, and S. Anand. 2011. *Bhimayana: Incidents in the Life of Bhimrao Ramji Ambedkar*. Navayana.

7

Graphic Narrative: An Innovative Tool to Educate and Inspire

Darakhshan Niyaz

In today's tech-savvy, audio-visual world, everything has become fast-paced. Right from accessing information on news, recipes, politics, fashion and weather to ordering cuisines, booking tickets, paying bills, doing business and conducting online classes and webinars, all are merely a few clicks of buttons away. Though these have contributed to our skyrocketing progress in this century, at the same time, they have transformed us all into highly restless and impatient beings. Also, these technological advancements have taken a toll on our general health. Another major turnaround has been regarding the fast-receding interest in the world of printed words, the books. Once considered a storehouse of knowledge, mysteries and window to the chiaroscuro world, books have long abated their appeal in the present times. This dwindling number of readers can be attributed to twofold facts—firstly, the alluring technicolour macrocosm of technology and secondly, the seemingly dreary cosmos of texts and tracts.

However, this isn't exactly the beginning of a child's tryst with books. When the children are introduced to their primers for the first time, their faces light up at the sight of colourful pictures of people, places and things. For them, an entirely disparate array of stimuli opens up, stimulating their sensibilities and stirring up their thoughts. It is as if these books do all the talking, keeping their little listeners rapt. At first, these colourful renderings are trickled with just a few words or phrases to introduce the pupil to language—one of the most powerful tools that humanity ever devised. Slowly yet progressively, these tiny troops of ink begin to dominate the pages, driving the sketches to a corner and finally dismissing them altogether from the sheets of the tome! This entire process, though gradual, does not escape the eyes of the students. Their once dazzling and dearly loved companions turn into nondescript monotonous mates. This very well explains our lifelong fondness for comic strips, books and magazines. At the same time, this also describes the reluctant attitude that the students develop towards these somewhat heavy and drab artefacts.

From the above-detailed discussion, the moot point driven home is that in this multimedia-crazy environment, students find it quite difficult to concentrate and imbibe knowledge from books. Their scientific temper and natural inquisitiveness toward novelties also wane off. With this picture in focus, there has been a serious discussion among the academicians about devising how students can be successfully weaned away from such diversions and brought back to the book house. One such step in this direction is the full-fledged welcoming of graphic books into the education system. The graphic books, as the name suggests, are the outcome of coalescing pictorial and alphabetic characters into a single frame.

The history of graphic books can be traced back to the cave paintings by early humans or to the hieroglyphics by ancient Egyptians. But these were prevalent in those times when human beings had not invented written language; hence recorded all their information by using these symbols and signs. With the advent of the complicated system of writing, human civilisation progressed by leaps and bounds, turning its back on these abstract images of the past. However, the idea behind resorting to the illustration on a large scale does not mean a retrogressive development. It is aimed at combining the best of both worlds. It is this tremendous potential of graphic novels that the Central Board of Secondary Education (CBSE) intends to harness in the Indian education system. The task of evolving more than a hundred graphic novels based on the books published by the National Council of Educational Research and Training

(NCERT) is already underway, taken up by around fifty CBSE schools throughout India (Chakravarty 2021). The chapters are divided into several topics, supported by illustrations, followed by worksheets. This kind of comprehensive approach to a particular topic would motivate the students to learn as against the usual pedagogical methods of teaching and learning. The entire job of developing the texts into graphic books is being done by the teachers and students themselves. This helps in keeping up with the taste, choice as well as mental maturity of the students. It is very similar to almost recreating the text again as the novel issues of gender equality, casteism, communal harmony, inclusiveness of women and more have been introduced and are dealt with great dexterity and expertise. All this would help in moulding the young budding minds for the betterment of their future as well as society.

One of the pioneering critical works in this field is the book titled *The Indian Graphic Novel: Nation, History and Critique* (2016) by Pramod K. Nayar. It is a detailed study of Indian graphic novels, which is considered a subset of South Asian graphic literature. Nayar assertively says that graphic narrative has an edge over the other genres as it keeps the readers simultaneously engaged in the act of reading and discerning. He emphasises the still untapped potential of this genre in Indian English literature as well as history. Nayar points out that the duality of narration is offered to us through this genre. Nayar optimistically asserts that an Indian graphic novel possesses all the qualifications of a literary text. It champions the Indian graphic narrative as "a new representational mode that re-invigorates the canon of Indian writing in English" (7–8). Another important aspect of graphic fiction, as pointed out by Nayar, is that there is no history outside modes of representation of a graphic novel. As a result, the role of graphic novels is all the more pertinent as lesser-known people, events or places that haven't been documented or properly depicted in history books so far find representation through this medium. Nayar (2016) argues, "It is essential to see popular forms and their demotive registers as enabling the culturization of the public sphere, opening it up to concerns, debates and campaigns about rights, historical wrongs, and emancipator possibilities" (198). One such example is a graphic text titled *A Gardener in the Wasteland: Jyotiba Phule's Fight for Liberty* (2012), authored by Srividya Natrajan and illustrated by Aparajita Ninan. It narrates the war waged on the partisan religious system by Jyotirao Govindrao Phule that consecrated the Brahmanical sect as opposed to the Sudras and Atisudras, who were subjected to extreme exploitation and ostracisation.

In the context of Indian literary taste, the graphic comic book *Amar Chitra Katha* launched in 1967, has been quite a popular choice among children as well as adults. It presented history intermingled with legends and mythologies aimed at entertaining as well as educating the readers at the same time. Taking a cue from these, several Indian graphic novels followed suit. One of these worth mentioning is *Hush* (2011) by Pratheek Thomas, illustrated by Rajiv Eipe, a silent mini graphic novel devoid of words. It illustrates the story of a schoolgirl who is a victim of child sex abuse. Another graphic text relevant to present times is *Drawing the Line: Indian Women Fight Back* (2015), published by feminist Indian publisher Zubaan Books and the Goethe Institute. It is an anthology comprising fourteen graphic stories that deal with everyday discrimination and violence faced by women. The anthology was conceptualised in response to the brutal Delhi gang rape case of 2012. *This Side, That Side: Restorying Partition* (2013) is yet another anthology comprising twenty-eight stories published by Yoda Press with the support of the Goethe Institute.

A graphic novel based on the biography of Dr. Bhimrao Ambedkar, titled *Bhimayana: Experiences of Untouchability* (2011), collaboratively penned down by Srividya Natrajan and S. Anand, portrays the plight of untouchables in India through Ambedkar's life and struggles. It incorporates some unique and innovative features within itself. With regard to illustrations by Durgabal and Subhash Vyam, it employs Gond artists. It fuses folk art tradition into the modern elements of a graphic novel. Another distinctive feature is the employment of thought balloons that function as the mind's eye. It is of two kinds—speech balloons shaped like birds and words of cruelty, where the balloon's tail is transformed into a scorpion's sting. These thought balloons convey the feelings as well as the theme of the novel, while different fonts are used for diverse emotions. *Bhimayana* shows the freedom that an artist can exercise in this novel. This also shows the various avenues that this mode of fiction opens in the field of fictional narratives. As assertively put by Nayar in his book, *The Indian Graphic Novel: Nation, History and Critique* (2016),

> The Indian graphic narrative must be seen as a part of a global 'graphic turn' to stories of disaster, disease, deprivation and displacement, stories that constitute the foundational texts of global campaigns for rights, equality and an end to suffering. Thus, the Indian graphic narrative is poised to become a part of the global popular, taking specific local contexts and conditions of casteism or abuse via a globally hypervisible and widely recognized medium, onto the world readership screens (196–197).

Orijit Sen's *River of Stories* (1994), published by Kalpavriksha, deals with the controversial Narmada Bachao Andolan spearheaded against the displacement of millions of people due to the construction of dams on the river Narmada. Vishwajyoti Ghosh's *Delhi Calm* (2010) decoded the tumultuous times of The Emergency imposed on India. The graphic novels *Kari* (2008) by Amrita Patil and *Corridor* (2004) by Sarnath Banerjee have a common urban backdrop and explore complicated relationships through a lesbian community and liaisons based on modern love, respectively.

Among the above-listed graphic novelists, Sarnath Banerjee, a professionally accomplished expert in image and communication, has a series of books to his credit like—*Corridor* (2004), *The Barn Owl's Wondrous Capers* (2007), *The Harappa Files* (2011) and *All Quiet in Vikaspuri* (2015). His work is a mixture of autobiography, true events, fictionalised versions of stories rooted in the middle-class struggle and beliefs and narratives based on political whims, vendetta, malpractices, short-sightedness and so on. Through his works, he intends to reveal the real, throbbing nation beneath the veneer of a new, vibrant India.

One more creative writing worth mentioning is *Longform: An Anthology of Graphic Narratives* (2018). It is the handiwork of four specialists in the field of graphic books—Sarabjit Sen, Debkumar Mitra, Pinaki Dey and Sekhar Mukherjee. It strongly advocates a serious consideration for this genre on a larger scale in the Indian literary scene. It includes a collection of stories having varied styles illustrated by thirty graphic artists.

Though graphic novels are not considered to be an altogether separate genre (as it comes within the ambit of fiction works), still the amalgamation of images and statements makes it a unique multipronged tool. These graphic narratives can be used to sensitise the students:

- Regarding environmental issues like global warming, air pollution, rising sea level, maintaining general cleanliness and so on.
- About gender issues, including gender equality, breaking gender stereotypes, girl child education and likewise.
- For eradication of superstition, orthodox ideas and obsolete practices, thereby developing scientific temper.
- Towards the well-being of elderlies, viewing them as guides and mentors rather than a burden.
- Uprooting communal, caste, religious and regional differences by introducing the students to the diversified lifestyle and cultural practices of people from all over the country.
- Helping to strengthen unity and the sense of belongingness to the nation.

There is a boundless scope of graphic novels; their full potential needs to be recognised and put into practice, such as:

- These graphic books, when carefully constructed keeping in view of the needs and capabilities of dyslexic readers, can help them tremendously.
- It would prove to be a boon for reluctant readers who might otherwise drop out of school.
- Graphic books can greatly assist students in learning a foreign language, making it an interesting endeavour.

- Graphic books and narratives can also contribute to the field of healthcare by spreading awareness on hygiene and can be effective in disseminating information on lifestyle diseases like diabetes, obesity, stress-related ailments and so on.
- Since the conversion of books into graphic ones is already underway, it has opened up new avenues for employment for numerous artists and paved the way for future students of fine arts.

As every new policy or idea has its pros and cons, similarly, these graphic texts have their share of drawbacks:

- It is feared that the language and reading efficiency of students would be hampered.
- It is believed to be inimical to the development of reading and writing skills of the students of primary level.
- Not all textbooks or subjects (for example, mathematics, science, philosophy and so on) offer themselves fully to being converted to graphic forms.
- Paper consumption will tend to increase. The cost of printing, the role of the illustrator, the use of colours and so on will only add up to the total publication cost of such books, making it in turn unaffordable to the children belonging to the economically backward section of society.
- Though these novels sell well, they are far from being bestsellers, partly due to their high prices and partly because of their inaccessibility to the common people.

The strength, as well as success of these graphic books, lie in the fact that, unlike the mostly pedantic textbooks, these 'texts' are absorbing and engaging. It is this juxtaposition of pictures and texts that would draw the readers towards itself, thus enabling it to create a niche for itself in the field of education. These graphic narratives would empower educators, teachers and academicians to achieve the long-sought-after targets of reducing dropout rates among students, standardising and bringing uniformity in academic levels across schools all over the country. Another important aspect of these graphic texts is their co-curricular nature, which is relevant across different curricula, thus adding multiple layers of interpretations for students to discover. However, before pursuing targets, it is highly imperative to reduce the cost of publication to make it easier and equally accessible to all. These graphic books need to broaden their scope to include higher education too in their purview. Also, the instructors or teachers would have to undergo the requisite training so that they can seriously engage the students in this pursuit. They need to have prior knowledge of the use of colours, angles, framing, foregrounding and more in these works—very similar to the techniques used in motion pictures. The teachers would have to be wary about their approach towards these and abstain from relying heavily on the printed words within the graphic fiction, thus, allowing a window to open for free interpretation by the students. Instead of putting the tag of non-serious and less literary on them, these can be equally rewarding for the students of senior grades if properly evolved. One such step in this direction is the coming up of progressive graphic novels, a term coined by Paul Gravett in his article *The Indian Graphic Novel is Here to Stay* (2015)

> It relies less on the corporate conveyer belt production system of editors, writers, pencillers inkers, colorists and letterers. They are often the work of a single auteur or a close partnership working as one. Being in control of every task brings a greater personality, directness and intimacy as one person or a collaborative duo can put their thoughts and feelings into words and pictures (Gravett 2015).

The real power of these books is that they aim toward developing a positive relationship with their disciples because when learning is not forced, it becomes a pleasure.

Works Cited

Banerjee, Sarnath. 2001. *The Barn Owl's Wondrous Capers*. New Delhi: Penguin Books India.

———. 2004. *Corridor*. New Delhi: Penguin Books India.

———. 2011. *The Harappa Files*. New Delhi: Harper Collins.

———. 2015. *All Quiet in Vikaspuri*. New Delhi: Harper Collins.

Chakravarty, Apoorva. 2021. "Here's How 50 Indian CBSE Schools Are Developing 120 Graphic Novels Based On NCERT Books." ScooNews. March 15, 2021. https://scoonews.com/news/news-here-s-how-50-indian-cbse-schools-are-developing-120-graphic-novels-based-on-ncert-books-10489/.

Ghosh, Vishwajyoti. 2010. *Delhi Calm*. New Delhi: Harper Collins.

———. 2013. *This Side, That Side: Restorying Partition : Graphic Narratives from Pakistan, India, Bangladesh*. New Delhi: Yoda Press.

Gravett, Paul. 2015. "The Indian Graphic Novel Is Here to Stay." British Council. October 29, 2015. https://www.britishcouncil.org/voices-magazine/indian-graphic-novel-here-stay.

Kuriyan, Priya, Larissa Bertonasco, and Ludmilla Bartscht, eds. 2015. *Drawing the Line: Indian Women Fight Back!* Zubaan.

Natarajan, Srividya. 2011. *A Gardener in the Wasteland: Jotiba Phule's Fight for Liberty*. Navayana.

Nayar, Pramod K. 2016. *The Indian Graphic Novel: Nation, History and Critique*. London: Routledge. https://openlibrary.org/books/OL29388065M/Indian_Graphic_Novel.

Patil, Amruta. 2008. *Kari*. New Delhi: Harper Collins.

Sen, Orijit. 1994. *The River of Stories*. Kalpavriksha.

Sen, Sarbajit, and Debkumar Mitra, eds. 2018. *Longform: An Anthology of Graphic Narratives*. Harper Collins.

Thomas, Pratheek, and Rajiv Eipe. 2010. *Hush: Some Things Are Not Meant to Be Talked About*. Manta Ray Comics.

Vyam, Durgabai, Srividya Natarajan, Subhash Vyam, and S. Anand. 2011. *Bhimayana: Incidents in the Life of Bhimrao Ramji Ambedkar*. Navayana.

8

Graphic Narratives: An Emerging Source of Education for Learners

Ritu Pareek

Introduction

Graphic novels and comic books have traditionally been seen as a kind of entertainment for both children and adults. However, because of their widespread impact, this media might very well be used as a teaching tool (Schwarz 2006; Mallia 2007; Tatalovic 2009). The findings of interviews performed with middle school English instructors to examine their understanding, viewpoints and willingness to use graphic novels as instructional material to teach ESL learners in Indian classrooms will be presented in this study.

English teachers from middle school were interviewed from three schools in Mumbai that were associated with three separate education boards, which are Rajasthan Board, CBSE, and ICSE Board. Most of them expressed reservations about the use of graphic novels in classrooms. Lack of familiarity, insufficient training and the incorporation of graphic novels into the current traditional curriculum were among the issues. Policymakers and teacher educators must take these concerns seriously to foster the appropriate usage of comics and graphic novels in the Indian ESL context.

Comics and Graphic Novels Development in India

The fables of *Panchatantra*, written around the third century BCE, were used to teach politics and leadership to the king's successors. They are, in a true sense, the earliest reference to aided learning in India. Comic books have been popular reading material for children in the last three decades, though not in a serious way. *Diamond Comics*, *Amar Chitra Katha* and other similar publications have established extensive distribution networks across the country and are read by thousands of children in a variety of languages. As a result, the graphic novel has arisen as a viable alternative for both children and adults, integrating a wide range of themes, including well-known classics.

McCloud in his book *Understanding Comics* (1993) defines graphic narrative as, "Juxtaposed pictorial and other imagery in planned sequence, designed to impart information and/or to entertain" (9). India's first graphic novel, *River of Stories* by Orijit Sen, was published in 1994. However, in 2004, Sarnath Banerjee's *Corridor* became India's first commercially successful English-language graphic novel. The popularity of graphic novels has skyrocketed since then. Some of the well-known Indian graphic novels are *The Barn Owl's Wondrous Capers* (2007), *Kari* (2008), *Private-Eye Anonymous: The Art Gallery Case* (2008), *Hotel at the End of the World* (2009), *Moonward* (2009) and *A Gardener in the Wasteland* (2011) to name a few.

With the advent of new exclusive comics publishers like Vimanika Comics (2008), Campfire Graphic Novels and Holy Cow Entertainment (2011) the industry of Indian graphic novel publication has broadened significantly in recent years. Campfire Graphic Novels, which began publishing in 2008, specialises in graphic novels based on Indian mythology, biography, classics and other creative stories. "Today, roughly 15-20 of our novels are a part of the CBSE extra-curriculum study list," Girija Jhunjhunwala, director of Campfire Graphic Novels, said in an article in *Print Week* magazine. As a result, "the books are not only suggested in schools and picked up by teachers but they are also recognised by educational boards such as the CBSE." She also mentions that the Kendriya Vidyalaya Sangathan has picked up twelve of their titles. Both the CBSE and the Kendriya Vidyalaya recommend titles like *Mother Teresa: Angel of the Slums* (2013), *Conquering Everest: The Lives of Edmund*

Hillary and Tenzing Norgay (2012), *Sundarkaand: Triumph of Hanuman* (2012) and more to be included in the curriculum. (Kumar 2016)

The popularity of this genre has sparked a new wave of comics cafes and libraries in India, particularly in Delhi, Bangalore and Mumbai. The first Annual Comics Convention in India, held in 2011, was dedicated to putting on a one-of-a-kind event and providing a forum for fans, exhibitors, and partners of the medium to interact. This convention has been held every year since then. Given the significant influence of comics and graphic novels on both children and adults, this medium has the potential to serve as both a source of amusement and an effective instructional tool.

The Graphic Novel as a Teaching Aid

"In comic strips, the emotional role of instructions is highlighted, with the goal of attracting and motivating less-able learners" (Hartley 1994, 87). Comics/graphic novels are thought to increase enjoyment while also encouraging the use of other aspects that might aid cognition (Mallia 2007). Many scholars believe that comics function as decoration by captivating pupils and pushing them to read (Bell and Gower 1998; Goldstein 2008; Hill 2003; Prowse 1998; Romney and Bell 2012; Viney 2006). According to research (Liu 2004, 226), providing pupils with a visual depiction of words can assist them in overcoming and understanding issues (Gyselinck and Tardieu 1999). Many classes employ visuals to help students understand what they are reading. Paivio's dual coding hypothesis explains the positive effect of multimodal texts on comprehension (Liu 2004, 752). Human cognition, according to Paivio, consists of two subsystems that process knowledge at the same time: one processing verbal information and the other visual information (Sadoski and Paivio 2001). When students are presented with a written text accompanied by images rather than a written text alone, both the visual and verbal systems are activated and integrated, allowing them to make conclusions about the content (Sadoski and Paivio 2001).

Comics and graphic novels are gradually gaining acceptance as a genre of literature. However, in India, research on graphic novels and their instructional applications is still in its infancy. In the classroom, employing them as resources can provide variation to the conventional curriculum and encourage self-reading. Furthermore, even a reluctant student will find them simple to understand. Let us now investigate Indian teachers' perspectives on the use of graphic novels in language instruction.

Methodology

We sought to see if this popular kind of amusement is now being used for language education, as well as assess the instructor's understanding, opinions and willingness to experiment with a form of text such as graphic novels that are distinct from the normally required texts. We will also look at what kind of help teachers might require while implementing these tools in the classroom. Our study's fieldwork included informal, one-on-one semi-structured interviews with instructors from the schools chosen for the study. The information gathered was analysed to see what the participants thought about using graphic novels in the classroom. In the following parts, we will go through the specifics of how this study was carried out.

This study included English language teachers from different schools. The teachers were between the ages of twenty-eight and fifty-four, with a range of four to twenty-nine years of school teaching experience. All the teachers were middle school teachers, meaning they taught at least one or more of classes VI, VII or VIII if not all of them. Every instructor held advanced degrees in their field. The teachers came from three different schools, each of which was affiliated with one of the city's three main boards, namely CBSE (Central Board of Secondary Education), RB (Rajasthan Board) and ICSE (Indian Certificate of Secondary Education). There were sixteen pre-determined problems highlighted during the interview. These include information regarding the grades the teachers taught, their teaching experience, educational credentials, age, their opinions on the current classroom materials and the learners' reactions to these materials. Teachers' acquaintance with graphic novels, including perspectives on using fantasy novels for language education in middle school and other topics were also discussed. Other questions arose throughout the discussion with the participants in terms of the opinion of teachers.

Currently, the available school textbooks contain works of literature with few drawings and limited colour. Ninety percent of the teachers stated that the mandated resources (main reader and workbook) being used in class were uninteresting and that the learners' reception to them was mostly unenthusiastic. According to one teacher, manuals should be more vibrant because colours affect pupils of all ages. Approximately sixty percent of the teachers stated that the students are bored in class since the book appears to be very uninteresting. They stressed the necessity of including relevant graphics in textbooks to help students better engage with the content. Their present textbooks lacked these images. Another quarter of the teachers said their pupils preferred short stories to big storybooks and that they were more willing to conduct film adaptations of classic novels than read them. Only twenty percent of the teachers thought the present texts were adequate.

When asked what may be used in addition to the mandated materials, most teachers preferred films (seventy-eight percent) accompanied by PowerPoint slides (sixty percent) and activity-based learning (twenty percent). Only twenty percent of the teachers believed graphic novels have been used in the classroom. This reaction was not surprising, given that most teachers were unfamiliar with the graphic book genre: only five teachers (twenty-five percent) were familiar with at least one. Only one instructor had read a graphic novel.

Participants were asked if they had ever employed graphic novels in a classroom activity or as a component of a lesson plan. While eighty-five percent of the teachers said they had never taught with a comic strip, fifteen percent said they had delivered a lesson from the CBSE Class VI book that was in the style of a comic strip. Unawareness of the genre, lack of knowledge of the accessibility of these novels on the market and lack of training when using graphic novels as teaching devices are some of the reasons for teachers to not include graphic novels inside the classroom. Some of the teachers expressed a desire for ready-made teaching resources, such as graphic novel-style textbooks with reading exercises and other relevant activities. A practical problem with using fantasy novels in the curriculum was the cost of purchasing them for the entire class, as these volumes required reading and most families would be hesitant to pay for them. Teachers also saw a need for assistance on how to select appropriate graphic novels to fit the mandated curriculum for various grades. Some of the teachers stated that they had never considered using graphic novels to teach.

The answers of the instructors who had delivered the comic strip-style lesson echoed each other. They said the students were engaged in the session and appreciated the activities that were set up around it. Teachers were asked if they would like graphic novels to be required in reading. Out of the twenty instructors polled, eighteen (ninety percent) were enthusiastic about the notion. Graphic novels, they believed, would be much more effective teaching tools than textbooks. They believed that current textbooks were boring. Using comics and graphic novels would pique the interest of struggling students and inspire them to discuss the characters and artwork in the comics. This medium may eventually be useful for language instruction. Some teachers advised that the supplementary reader, out of the two volumes required for the school curriculum, be a graphic novel because pictures performed much better than text alone. They also suggested that graphic novels be utilised to improve language abilities by using dialogue, implicit speech, subject-verb agreement and other techniques.

However, teachers identified several concerns that should be considered before adopting fantasy novels in the curriculum. They are as follows:

- Due to the great motivation to complete the entire syllabus, there is insufficient time to add advanced techniques such as graphic novels.

- Students in classes VIII and up believe they are too advanced for comics and would rather read serious literature than drawings for fear of being seen as infantile.
- Students' English levels may suffer because of the so-called simple language employed in comics.
- It could be better to give the pupils something more difficult than comics because comics provide illustrations and the students' creativity may take a back seat in terms of learning.

Overall, while teachers were receptive to utilising graphic novels as supplemental tools in addition to conventional courses, they were not in favour of graphic novels replacing regular textbooks. They also believed that certain components of English could not have been taught by graphics or graphic novels; for example, they questioned if poetry could be conveyed through comics and claimed that poetry could only be taught through a textbook.

Discussion

The outcomes of this study clearly show that, in urban areas, a huge majority of teachers are amenable to the notion of employing comics/graphic novels as educational tools. Many teachers were dissatisfied with the current materials and believed that there was room for more materials such as films, PowerPoint presentations and activity-based learning. Although some teachers recognised graphic novels as a possible motivator for pupils, there were additional pedagogical benefits that needed to be identified and teachers trained properly.

Teachers believed that preservice as well as training was essential to address the issues expressed previously in the study. The school administration must also play a vital role in providing training to teachers on how to effectively use graphic novels in the classroom. Furthermore, educational policymakers should encourage instructors to adopt graphic novels by putting them in the curriculum, either as supplemental reading or by adapting some courses to a visual format.

There are some drawbacks to this study. We used a tiny sample size of people of the same gender from only one location, with no input from other stakeholders such as parents, institutional policymakers, administrators or, of course, students. Our conclusions would have been much more comprehensive if we had a broader group of people from various backgrounds. Nonetheless, the current research provides information into the perspectives of a subset of teachers.

Works Cited

Appupen. 2009. *Moonward: Stories from Halahala*. India: Blaft.

Banerjee, Sarnath. 2004. *Corridor*. Penguin Books India.

———. 2007. *The Barn Owl's Wondrous Capers*. Penguin Books India.

Bell, Jan, and Roger Gower. 1998. "Writing Course Materials for the World: a Great

Compromise." In *Materials Development in Language Teaching*, edited by Brian Tomlinson, 116–29. Cambridge: Cambridge University Press. doi:10.1017/9781139042789.008.

Goldstein, Ben. 2008. *Working with Images*. Cambridge University Press.

Gyselinck, Valérie, and Hubert Tardieu. 1999. "The Role of Illustrations in Text Comprehension: What, When, for Whom, and Why?" In *The Construction of Mental Representations During Reading*, edited by Herr Van Oostendorp and Susan R. Goldman, 195–218. https://psycnet.apa.org/record/1998-06740-008.

Hartley, James. 1994. *Designing Instructional Text*. Kogan.

Helfand, Lewis. 2011. *Conquering Everest: The Lives of Edmund Hillary and Tenzing Norgay: A Graphic Novel*. Steerforth Press.

Helfand, Lewis, and Sachin Nagar. 2013. *Mother Teresa: Angel of the Slums*. Campfire Graphic Novels.

Hill, David A. 2003. "The Visual Element in EFL Course Books." In *Developing Materials for Language Teaching*, edited by Brian Tomlinson, 174–82. Continuum.

Kumar, Rahul. 2016. "Telling Stories in Graphics." *Print Week*, July 13, 2016. http://www.printweek.in/features/telling-storiesgraphics-20953.

Liu, Jun. 2004. "Effects of Comic Strips on L2 Learners' Reading Comprehension." *TESOL Quarterly* 38 (2): 225–43. https://doi.org/10.2307/3588379.

Mallia, Ġorġ. 2007. "Learning from the Sequence: The Use of Comics in Instruction." *University of Florida* 3 (3). https://imagetextjournal.com/learning-from-the-sequence-the-use-of-comics-in-instruction/.

McCloud, Scott. 1993. *Understanding Comics*. Harper Perennial.

Modak, Tejas. 2008. *Private-Eye Anonymous: The Art Gallery Case*. Westland.

Nagar, Sachin, Shyam Prakash, and Tulsidas. 2012. *Sundarkaand: Triumph of Hanuman*. Campfire.

Natarajan, Srividya. 2011. *A Gardener in the Wasteland: Jotiba Phule's Fight for Liberty*. Navayana.

Patil, Amruta. 2007. *Kari*. India: Harper Collins.

Prowse, Philip. 1998. "How Writers Write: Testimony from Authors." In *Materials Development in Language Teaching*, edited by Brian Tomlinson, 130–45. Cambridge University Press.

Romney, Cameron and Leon Bell. 2012. "The Role of Graphics in Business English

Textbooks". *The 2011 Pan-SIG Conference Proceedings* edited by Kim. Bradford-Watts, Robert Chartrand and Eric M. Skier, 210–219.

Sadoski, Mark, and Allan Paivio. 2001. *Imagery and Text: A Dual Coding Theory of Reading and Writing*. https://ci.nii.ac.jp/ncid/BB1392121X.

Schwarz, Gretchen. 2006. "Expanding Literacies through Graphic Novels." *English Journal* 95 (6): 58–64. https://doi.org/10.2307/30046629.

Sen, Orijit. 1991. *The River of Stories*. India: Kalpavriksha.

Singh, Parismita. 2009. *The Hotel at the End of the World*. Penguin Books.

Tatalovic, Mico. 2009. "Science Comics as Tools for Science Education and Communication: A Brief, Exploratory Study." *Journal of Science Communication* 08 (04). https://doi.org/10.22323/2.08040202.

Viney, Peter. 2006. "How NOT to Write Really Rotten Materials." *Modern English Teacher* 15 (3). https://peterviney.com/about/elt-articles/how-not-to-write-%E2%80%A6/.

9

Animals as Visual Metaphors in Graphic Narratives

Sapna Dogra

Animal characters abound in graphic narratives. On celluloid, they are very common. For many graphic artists, anthropocentrism is a literary technique that achieves an ecstatic outcome. The anthropocentrism adds to the aesthetic presentation—establishing structure and agency that generates and constructs an interspace from the real, a distance that furnishes necessary space for the reader. Animals and their anthropomorphism in cartoons and graphic art have become part of our collective consciousness. According to Mayersen (2018), "the use of animal imagery in graphic novels gives the author the power to communicate with a subtlety and emotive command not otherwise readily available" (167).

Walt Whitman (1885) in one of his popular poems, *Animals*, says:

> I think I could turn and live with animals, they are so placid and self-contain'd,
>
> I stand and look at them long and long.
>
> They do not sweat and whine about their condition,
>
> They do not lie awake in the dark and weep for their sins,
>
> They do not make me sick discussing their duty to God,
>
> Not one is dissatisfied, not one is demented with the mania of owning things,

> Not one kneels to another, nor to his kind that lived thousands of years ago,
>
> Not one is respectable or unhappy over the whole earth. (79)

As a witness to slavery, racism and civil war, Whitman's misanthropism is understandable. He appreciates and admires the humility and modesty of animals which he feels to be amiss in the human race. He considers animals to be selfless creatures free of earthly desires. According to the poet, animals do not whine, weep or despise their plight. They draw no pleasure in being above others and pulling others down. They have no mania for wealth and material well-being. The poem becomes an extended annotation to the question—why is it easier to make a point using animal characters, rather than their human counterpart?

As early as 550 BC, Aesop wrote his famous fables and parables about animal characters with human characteristics. These were possibly the first stories with this element in Western literature. Aesop deployed this technique of animals as visual metaphors to put together short moral lessons in his stories. This made his works more accessible to readers. It is thought that animal-themed comics and cartoons are said to have originated in fables and fairy tales. In India, anthropocentrism has been used in *The Panchatantra* and *The Jataka*. In Indian and Greek mythology, humans would morph into animals and vice-versa. On television, they are integral to cartoons, thanks to Walt Disney. If there's one literary genre where animals are ubiquitous, it is graphic narratives.

Maus

Art Spiegelman published the first volume of this Holocaust graphic novel, *Maus I* in 1986 and *Maus II* in 1991. *Maus* recounted the tale of Spiegelman's father, Vladek Spiegelman, an Auschwitz survivor. The narrative moves back and forth between World War II-era Poland and New York in the 1970s. It is the only graphic novel that has ever won the Pulitzer Prize. The quote "The Jews are undoubtedly a race, but they are not human" by Hitler inspired Spiegelman to write *Maus*. Touted as a daringly political novel, *Maus* uses the imagery of mice as Jews, cats as Nazis, dogs as Americans, French as frogs and the Swedes as reindeers. Meyersen points out that "Yet *Maus* was not the first to use animal imagery to depict genocide within this format. French Jewish illustrator Horst Rosenthal produced a graphic booklet during the Holocaust that became one of Spiegelman's sources of inspiration. *Mickey Mouse in the Gurs Internment Camp* described daily life in the camp, portraying Mickey Mouse as a prisoner" (165). *Maus* unsettles its readers with the depiction of extreme violence. According to Haldule (2019),

> The devil's in the details, however—*Maus* doesn't merely elicit a response from the reader, it elicits the right response. After all, a human can be drawn with a range of expressions, but the micro-expressions in our features, easy enough to understand in real life, are difficult to pencil in. It's easier to use an animal's range of recognised habits—a swish of a cat's tail to indicate disgust, or a horse pacing in place to show he's restive.

The hierarchy of animals portrayed in *Maus* does not need explications as it is the exact order in the food chain too. It does not take long for the readers to identify the victimised and the victimiser. Spiegelman uses the reader's visual grammar which has been honed and fed with years of anthropomorphic art. As a result, the animal metaphor is crucial in this comic and it is, without a doubt, one of the primary reasons for its enormous success.

Animal characters in *Maus* acted more humanly than the animals they represented. Witek (1989) says that the animal comic "genre takes these allegorical meanings as a starting point but then proceeds to ignore, qualify, or reverse them" (110). Spiegelman chose animals to represent people from various countries around the world. It is very daring for him to illustrate the story of the holocaust and to use animals was venturesome.

Munnu: A Boy from Kashmir

Munnu: A Boy from Kashmir (2015) is an Indian graphic novel by Malik Sajad that recounts the story of a seven-year-old boy and his life in conflict-ridden Kashmir. The book can be categorised as a Bildungsroman, which refers to a coming-of-age story. In recognizably Spiegelmanian form, Sajad presents the Kashmiris as the critically endangered Hangul deer (or Kashmiri stag). According to Santesso (2020),

> Employing a "visual grammar" that echoes Art Spiegelman's anthropomorphic use of animals in *Maus*, Sajad illustrates Kashmiris as hanguls, an endangered species of deer. By emphasizing the vulnerability of the Kashmiris, Sajad delivers a critique of the random crackdowns, illegal detentions, and extrajudicial killings of a hegemonic state. The hanguls, in this sense, visually reinforce the idea of dehumanization experienced by those excluded from traditional human rights.

The novel becomes a scathing critique of religion, politics and politicised religious bigotry. According to Chaney (2011), one important reason for the use of animals as visual metaphors in graphic narratives is for "identity and otherness" (129). He further adds that the appearance of the animal in graphic novels "almost always accompanies the strategic and parodic veiling of the human" (130). Similarly, Alaniz (2019) opines that "As argued by John Berger, David Herman, and other scholars, the animal's lack of human speech renders it vulnerable to a brand of representational colonialism whereby its in-itself existence is emptied in favor of other symbolic, metaphorical, or ideological functions" (326). *Maus* humanised Jews by showing their everyday struggle, *Munnu* humanised Kashmiris as vulnerable.

Meyersen (2018) identifies two primary functions that non-anthropomorphised animals fulfil in graphic novels: "The Animal as Symbolic of the Human Condition" and "Animals as Emotional Cues" (170–176). He says,

> At times, animals play a strongly symbolic role, providing direct insight into the human condition. More commonly, they occupy a complex space in which they provide emotional cues to the reader. These cues provide important affective context. They immediately and effectively communicate emotion, removing some of the constraints

> to doing so in a medium in which written expression is inherently limited. They may cue emotional disruption, emotional calm, or positive or negative emotions. In this respect, animal imagery can offer a surprisingly flexible and functional trope. This may explain the relatively high prevalence of animal imagery within graphic novels about genocide (176).

Glenn Willmott (2011) points out that animal masks or bodies allowed for "*defamiliarization* of human traits—selfish violence perceived in wolves, innocence in songbirds, curiosity in cats . . . while in turn *naturalizing* these simplifications" (60). She goes on to explicate that "Nature, as now inferred by the comics readers, is no longer taxonomically stable or biologically recognizable; its normal classifications prove volatile. As a result, in modern comics, the defamiliarization-naturalization strategy of the animal fable genre henceforth defamiliarizes *both* human *and* animal under the alluringly stylized sign, however hermetic, of an inaccessible or uncertain nature at large" (60). The use of animals as visual metaphors also achieves the alienation effect as propounded by German playwright Bertot Brecht.

Bertolt Brecht (1898–1956) was a German playwright whose theatre was political and social. He is the leading theoretician of epic theatre. His theatre was a concerted effort to remind the audience of the play's theatricality. By disrupting the illusion of reality, he aimed to continuously shock and surprise his audience. He was a supporter of *Verfremdungseffekt,* which is often translated as alienation effect or estrangement but it is closely associated with distancing (Thomson and Sacks 2006). Brecht wanted his audiences to be engaged but not emotionally involved, expecting them to develop a critical perspective. Brecht introduced the concept of the Alienation effect in his essay, *Alienation Effects in Chinese Acting* (1964). The concept was derived from the Russian formalists and is "inseparable from the politics of modernism" (Blau 1989, 93). The use of animals creates a distance to look at the human side of the story by taking the focus away from 'the human' to the human. It generalises by distancing. The distance achieved by anthropomorphic animals according to Munk (2018), "is further amplified by the iconic drawings of the animals – their faces are drawn minimalistically, with very few differences from character to character, the only difference often being their clothing" (57).

The use of animals in graphic narratives distances them emotionally from problems that demand analytical and cerebral solutions. Like Brecht, most graphic novelists see little value in the realist depiction of characters and ideas. They like their readers to be observers and suspend their roles as participants.

Works Cited

Alaniz, José. 2019. "Animals in Graphic Narrative." In *The Oxford Handbook of Comic Book Studies*, edited by Frederick Luis Aldama, 326–34. Oxford University Press. https://doi.org/10.1093/oxfordhb/9780190917944.001.0001.

Blau, Herbert. 1989. "Receding into Illusion: Alienation, the Audience, Technique, Anatomy." *New German Critique*, no. 47 (January): 93–117. https://doi.org/10.2307/488109.

Brecht, Bertolt. 1964. "Alienation Effects in Chinese Acting." In *Brecht on Theatre: The Development of an Aesthetic*, edited and translated by John B. Willett, 91. Hill and Wang. http://ci.nii.ac.jp/ncid/BA29519583.

Chaney, Michael O. 2011. "Animal Subjects of the Graphic Novel." *College Literature* 38 (3): 129–49. https://doi.org/10.1353/lit.2011.0024.

Haldule, Tej. 2019. "More Human Than Humans: Exploring Animals In Graphic Novels." *The Curious Reader*, August. https://www.thecuriousreader.in/features/animals-in-graphic-novels/#:~:text=It's%20easier%20to%20make%20a,sympathy%20that%20the%20writer%20intends.

Joseph, Witek. 1989. "Comic Books as History: The Narrative Art of Jack Jackson, Art Spiegelman, and Harvey Pekar." *University Press of Mississippi* 27 (10). https://doi.org/10.5860/choice.27-5964.

Mayersen, Deborah. 2018. "Cockroaches, Cows and 'Canines of the Hebrew Faith': Exploring Animal Imagery in

Graphic Novels about Genocide." *Genocide Studies and Prevention: An International Journal* 12 (2): 165–78. https://doi.org/10.5038/1911-9933.12.2.1486.

Munk, Tea-Maria. 2018. "The Holocaust in Pictures: Maus and the Narrative of the Graphic Novel." *Leviathan: Interdisciplinary Journal in English*, no. 2 (March): 54–59. https://doi.org/10.7146/lev.v0i2.104696.

Sajad, Malik. 2015. *Munnu: A Boy From Kashmir*. HarperCollins UK.

Santesso, Esra Mirze. 2020. "One Page of the Graphic Novel Munnu: A Boy from Kashmir." *The National Endowment for the Humanities* 41 (1). https://www.neh.gov/article/one-page-graphic-novel-munnu-boy-kashmir.

Spiegelman, Art. 1986. *Maus: A Survivor's Tale*. New York: Pantheon Books.

Thomson, Peter C., and Glendyr Sacks. 2004. *The Cambridge Companion to Brecht. Cambridge University Press EBooks*. https://doi.org/10.1017/ccol0521414466.

Whitman, Walt. 2012. *Leaves of Grass 1855*. Pennsylvania: The Electronic Classics Series. https://edisciplinas.usp.br/pluginfile.php/3985648/mod_resource/content/1/LEAVES%20OF%20GRASS.pdf.

Willmott, Glenn. 2017. "The Animalized Character and Style." In *Animal Comics Multispecies Storyworlds in Graphic Narratives*, edited by David Herman. Bloomsbury Publishing.

10

Violence and Manipulation in *Kashmir Pending*

Sapna Dogra

The legendary Will Eisner coined the phrase graphic novel in 1964 and popularised it. The first graphic novel to capture the attention of the reading public was Art Spiegelman's Pulitzer Prize-winning *Maus*, published in 1986. The work told the story of World War II's Holocaust. The first graphic novel in India was *River of Stories* (1994), published by Kalpavriksha and written by Orijit Sen. Since then, the genre has come a long way in terms of representing the downtrodden and disenfranchised. Graphic novels, which differ from comics in terms of ideas and overall execution, are becoming increasingly popular among academic researchers. Naseer Ahmed's *Kashmir Pending* (2007) is a graphic novel about Mushtaq, a young man who joined the militant resistance against Indian control in Kashmir with high hopes and zeal but afterwards lost faith in the revolutionaries. The novel chronicles his consequent disillusionment, where he finally gives up hope and runs a tea stall. The novel narrates the story of numerous people in Kashmir and addresses regional unrest. It is a grim narrative that shows the futility of violence. The violence of manipulation that affects the young boys in Kashmir is the subtext that runs throughout. The young are unable to differentiate black from white and live in a perpetual state of doomed and unredeemed grey. The novel does not take recourse to the journalistic third person perspectives but presents facts from an insider's point of view where things are all in different shades of grey. With no perfect right or wrong, it is a narrative that moves towards an abysmal nothing. This book has received tons of praise from critics for its realistic portrayals of politics and psychology.

According to Hogan (2016), the three main reasons for addressing narratives of Kashmir currently are "the human importance of the crisis, the literary significance of the place, and the theoretically consequential nature of this somewhat atypical situation" (6). Mushtaq clearly has unsettled anger issues against the army, which is apparent from the first page itself. We meet him when he's not at home, but outside in public. At home, he is besieged by an unsupportive family that does not appreciate his artistic and creative abilities. At the university, he is smitten by the eloquence of the charismatic leaders of the Kashmir freedom movement. Under the influence of these speeches, he decides to go to a terrorist camp across the border for training. Disenchantment soon follows as he and the other fellows are not treated well. At the border, he bribes the guard with a wristwatch and makes his way back to the valley. More disenchantment and grief follow when he discovers that the militant recruiters are involved in the double-crossing conspiracy. He also loses his best friend in this process. The plot is fairly straightforward. The unrest in the valley, confused youth, and manipulation of youngsters who become puppets in the hands of larger forces are general themes one finds in any work of art based on Kashmir (Shashwata 2018).

The Visual and the Verbal

Kashmir Pending is a well-packed slim book with grim artwork. The title page explains that though the story is written by Naseer Ahmed, the visualization is by Saurabh Singh, Anindya Roy and Sarnath Banerjee. The artwork with generous use of reds and browns makes the narrative doubly daunting and quite disturbing. The book is verbally reticent but visually loquacious. The content is less prominent than the form and the medium. With a text around the unrest in the valley, one expects a textually dense and pedantic book, but *Kashmir Pending* is a breath of fresh air as it eschews verbal to the visual. There is always a danger of graphic novels becoming too textual and wordy. But in this case, it is a far cry from what the readers were expecting. The surreal zoom-ups and distant shots coupled with the harsh art style in *Kashmir Pending* create a lasting impact. The novel is populated with intense images of big brooding men in uniform and a lot of frightening shadows, successfully capturing the pathos of the place and moment in history. The story serves as a cautionary tale for future generations, discouraging them from joining the insurgency. According to Pan (2021), the red represents the "immediacy of violence and bloodshed in a perpetual warzone, and the monochrome symbolizes the bleakness of life under such circumstances." She further adds, "The use of speech bubbles is minimal, which is understandable as it is a recounted narrative rather than an immediately recorded one, whereby the details of conversations aren't of much consequence and it is the content and the consequent actions following the conversations that are retained in memory" (5). Similarly, Varughese (2017a) opines,

> Thinking of the graphic narrative as one which narrates a challenging story, coupled with dark and difficult visuals, is often recognised within western cultures as being of the graphic narrative mode. For India, however, where the visual especially has traditionally depicted and represented India (and Indianness) in positive and 'proper' ways, the advent of the post-millennial Indian graphic novel (and graphic narratives more broadly) has proved challenging to domestic Indian readerships, because ideas of Indianness have been portrayed in less favourable ways. Rather than bright, sharp, celebratory colourways, bold, clean line drawing and representation, Indian graphic narratives display sketch-like image, employ sepia and muted colour tones, alongside collage and mixed media elements for composition.

According to Dasgupta (2019), "But here's why you should go and get the book: the artwork. Saurabh Singh's dark and harsh portrayal of prisoners in cells, smoking, praying and talking set the tone brilliantly for the book. Making the cells shadowy, so that if it weren't for the bars, you'd think they were caves, gives the story a distinct no-nonsense look. Readers will also be reminded of *Sin City* in Singh's use of black and red." For the drawings in the novel, Desai (2011) adds, "The drawing in *Kashmir Pending* is documentary and iconic. Many panels are pointedly reminiscent of photographic stills familiar from headline stories, some an obvious outcome of freehand artwork by the artist Saurabh Singh based on photographs taken by the writer Nasser Ahmed. But the real highlight of this book is Saurabh Singh's artwork, in particular the many tenebrous images of prisoners sitting in shadowy cells, praying, passing cigarettes to each other, recounting their experiences, their sunken faces only half-visible (the artist makes very effective use of red and black)."

Clearly, the artwork of the novel lays bare the complex ways in which violence functions in Kashmir.

AFSPA: Disciplinary Institutions of Power and Monitoring

Kashmir Pending interrogates the disciplinary institutions of power and monitoring used by the Indian government. The issues that have been afflicting Kashmir for years are not new to most Indians. With the Armed Forces Special Powers Act (AFSPA), "troops could arrest, kill, or rough up any person on mere suspicion" (Ahmed 2007, 15). According to Morton (2022), such novels, "not only document the crossing of the Line of Control by so-called insurgents but also raise questions about the violence of state sovereignty by mourning the lives and deaths of those who dare to challenge the Indian state's spatial performance of sovereignty" (3). Visual repetition of images reinforces that "brutal techniques of governmentality have become normalized" (6). He further adds that if the AFSPA is formulated as a

> "temporary aberration" and a "mere enclave" in the dominant rhetoric of Indian nationalism, literary texts, films and memoirs can help to shed light on the violent techniques of military control and power that the government of India has employed to assert its sovereignty over the territory and area it deems to be disturbed. In so doing, such narratives can help to contest the liberal myth of India as a nation-state with an undifferentiated

> and representative democratic process. The techniques of military control that operate in contemporary Kashmir offer a powerful example of the disciplinary structures of power and surveillance that the government of India employs. (1–2)

The "testimonial force" (Morton 2022, 4) of such writings is not to be missed as such. According to Morton, "This use of a prison narrative to frame an analeptic sequence of visual and verbal story panels might encourage readers to view Kashmir Pending as a graphic novel that is critical of an Indian military that seeks to subjugate the Kashmiri population" (5–6). According to Hogan, "Indeed, one might go so far as to say that focusing on or foregrounding the agency of the militants and backgrounding government agency is part of the larger problematic that frames the conflict in a liberal version of standard colonial ideology" (112).

The plot of the book centres on several Kashmiri individuals who are trying to realize their goals and aspirations. The novel offers a counter-narrative and aids in dispelling the liberal idea that India is a nation-state with a uniform and representative democratic process. Such literary texts lay bare the violent tactics used by the military to assert its supremacy over the area it deems vulnerable and disturbed.

Stereotyping and Manipulation

Singh's *Kashmir Pending* refuses to take sides and presents the situation in Kashmir in shades of grey. While the Indian military is stereotyped, the populace is not bereft of the taint of mindless manipulation that they are victims of. The novel traces the life of a young man, who is a reformed militant. The story is narrated in the dark cells of a jail in Srinagar. What distinguishes him from others is his determination to bring about a change despite the anguish and alienation in the state. The novel depicts several characters in Kashmir and successfully captures the psyche of Kashmiris. Based on real characters, Ahmed sets his novel in militant-occupied Kashmir in 1989 to make a political case for the people of Kashmir. According to Shankar (2007),

> Singh's strokes and lines are powerful, invoking the horror of everyday Kashmir: guns, arrests, torture, betrayal and fundamentalism. Through its flash-frames, the tragic story of two friends who become terrorists takes on a haunted life of its own. There is no preaching here. What comes through is the very human message that the final victim is the terrorist himself, prey to the chimera that is today's Kashmir.

Shankar (2007) also adds that "It's obvious that the publisher Sarnath Banerjee, who authored India's first graphic novel *Corridor* has approached *Kashmir Pending* with the passion it deserves. It's noir's new beginning." One of the major motifs in the novel is violence. According to Varghese (2017b),

> The choice of the form of the graphic narrative to recount Kashmir Pending (2007) underscores the permeating forces of violence and death in conflict. The drawings depict the violence graphically and, moreover, the cycles of violence and death that are repeated in the narrative are demonstrated through the assemblage of the pages. The pictorial representations of anger and violence is juxtaposed with the silence and (comparative) calm which exist in both the prologue (the waters of Dal Lake) and the epilogue (the restaurant). The prologue-epilogue structure reinforces the sense of Mushtaq's journey (and Ali's to an extent) and, in turn, illustrates the idea that Kashmir is *pending*;, the violence continues around him, men still fight to free Kashmir, people continue to kill and die for the cause and, in this sense, the situation in Kashmir is cyclical (87).

The novel ends with Mushtaq giving up resistant politics in favour of a life of domestic peace as a tea-stall owner. It comes as a bit unsatisfactory. Readers and critics may find it too simplistic an ending. According to Pan (2012), "It is perhaps representative of the voice of a certain section of the general Kashmiri populace who feel trapped in the threefold contentions of India, Pakistan, and the militant revolutionaries who demand the independence of Kashmir and yearn peace" (8).

According to Hogan (2014), *Kashmir Pending* then "functions most obviously as a cautionary tale for potential militants, serving to dissuade them from taking part in the insurgency" (109).

Hogan also opines that "one of the most interesting and problematic aspects of the narrative is the way it treats the free choices of Kashmiri militants, the way it presents militants as making their own lives rather than being made by circumstances." (111) The novel fails to provide mnemonic counternarrative by refusing to go outside the official version of history (ies).

Conclusion

The subtext of *Kashmir Pending* is that the onus to end the vicious cycle of violence falls on the individuals of Kashmir. According to Desai (2011), "His story is also meant to be the story of Kashmir, personified, over the previous thirty-five or so tumultuous years." Mushtaq's declaration "I do not want any more innocent lives to be lost in the crossfires of my war" concludes the novel's idea of the futility of violence (Ahmed 2007, 95). Published by Phantomville (a publishing house exclusively for graphic novels, now inoperative), the novel has an intriguing title. According to Desai (2011), "Through Mushtaq, the novel, which is largely documentary in graphic format and execution, grapples with the issue of political impasse in contemporary Kashmir, namely that many Kashmiris want to secede. Specifically, then, Kashmir's political recognition as an autonomous state is what's 'pending' in the region, as it is in Ahmed and Singh's novel."

Works Cited

Ahmed, Naseer. 2007. *Kashmir Pending*. New Delhi: Phantomville.

"Armed Forces (Jammu and Kashmir) Special Powers Act, 1990." 1990. September 10, 1990. https://www.indiacode.nic.in/handle/123456789/1953? sam_handle=123456789/1362.

"Armed Forces Special Powers Ordinance." 1942. *Gazette of India Extraordinary*. https://www.mha.gov.in/sites/default/files/2023-04/AFSPA%201958_11042023_0.pdf.

Dasgupta, Anish. 2019. "Kashmir Pending — Naseer Ahmed." *Medium*, September 19, 2019. https://medium.com/9thart/kashmir-pending-naseer-ahmed-21487beccae1.

Desai, Prajna. 2011. "Kashmir Pending - The Comics Journal." The Comics Journal. November 18, 2011. http://www.tcj.com/reviews/kashmir-pending.

Hogan, Patrick Colm. 2014. "Kashmir Pending: Narrative and Ideology in a Graphic Novel." *Narrative Works*, July, 108–29. https://doi.org/10.7202/1062102ar.

———. 2016. *Imagining Kashmir: Emplotment and Colonialism*. USA: University of Nebraska Press. https://core.ac.uk/display/77945200.

Morton, Stephen. 2022. "Narratives of Mourning in the Shadow of the Armed Forces Special Powers Act: State Violence and Contested Sovereignty in Contemporary South-Asian Fiction." *University of Southampton* 17 (2 & 3): 1–22. https://www.postcolonial.org/index.php/pct/article/view/2733/2555.

Pan, Pratyusha. 2021. "Visual Art in Resistance: Examining Graphic Narratives as a Documentary of Social Realism through Analyses of Kashmir Pending and Palestine." *Presiuniv*, June. https://www.academia.edu/49281255/Visual_Art_in_Resistance_Examining_graphic_narratives_as_a_documentary_of_social_realism_through_analyses_of_Kashmir_Pending_and_Palestine.

Saha, Sashwata. 2018. "Noir: The Art of Darkness: A Look Into the Underrated Trove of Indian Noir Graphic Novels." *Media India Group*, September 17, 2018. https://mediaindia.eu/culture/noir-the-art-of-darkness/.

Shankar, Ravi. 2007. "'Kashmir Pending' Invocating the Horrors of Everyday Kashmir." *India Today*, April 30, 2007. https://www.indiatoday.in/magazine/society-the-arts/books/story/20070430-saurabh-singh-and-nasir-ahmed-releases-kashmir-pending-748743-2007-04-30.

Varughese, E. Dawson. 2017a. "Graphically Indian: Storying the Inauspicious (for Now) | IIAS." *The Study* 78 (11).

https://www.iias.asia/the-newsletter/article/graphically-indian-storying-inauspicious-now.

———. 2017b. *Visuality and Identity in Post-Millennial Indian Graphic Narratives*. *Springer EBooks*. India: Palgrave Macmillan Cham. https://doi.org/10.1007/978-3-319-69490-0.

Index